THE FREE AGENT MINDSET

THE FREE AGENT MINDSET

HOW CONTRARIANS ARE SHAPING THE FUTURE OF WORK

BY SCOTT JONES

NEW DEGREE PRESS

COPYRIGHT © 2020 SCOTT JONES

All rights reserved.

THE FREE AGENT MINDSET

How Contrarians are Shaping the Future of Work

ISBN   978-1-64137-981-6 *Paperback*

         978-1-64137-869-7 *Kindle Ebook*

         978-1-64137-870-3 *Ebook*

For Jessica, Mom, Dad, Carl & Todd

CONTENTS

———

INTRODUCTION

———

"The future ain't what it used to be."

— YOGI BERRA

It was a bright, humid as hell Tuesday morning in Washington, D.C. in the early summer of 2019.

Scootering with sweat pouring into my newly pressed navy blue suit, I was traveling on K Street, heading to my job as a financial consultant for a large brokerage firm downtown, a few blocks away from the White House.

Being home to some of the most powerful lawyers, lobbyists, and professionals in the world, you could smell the influence in the air – or rather the swamp that is a D.C summer arriving in full swing.

The journey through the bustling streets was always an exciting one. Weaving around the frenzy of people crossing the street in their usual morning panic, sounds of trumpets and makeshift drums, and, of course, hundreds of cars honking their horns with full vengeance.

Like most mornings, I decided to pull into a local coffee shop before beginning my day.

Very few smells are as satisfying as the aroma of freshly brewed coffee, and the sound of an espresso machine steaming milk has become music to my ears.

I stood in the line full of impatient, dark suits and skirts, all with a bit of sweat glistening across their foreheads, ready to purchase their regular coffee. A quick turn to the right, past the pack of suits, were a few people wearing jeans and t-shirts, complete with a MacBook on the table next to their mugs.

They looked comfortable. And dry.

They had also come fully equipped with water, supplies, and a breakfast sandwich or some sort of pastry.

They were here to stay.

Wiping my damp forehead with my backpack strap and having the appearance of someone after running a marathon, I asked myself, "how do I get to be one of those people?"

It wasn't immediately, but over time that question weighed on me more and more. I was bored with my job, and my career was heading to a place where I didn't want it to go, a place that would be difficult to come back from.

How do you make that change?

With what was an extremely difficult decision of mine, I wound up leaving my full-time job at the end of that summer.

This of course was the pre-COVID-19 world. The economy was booming, the job market was at all-time lows, and you could still sit down in a coffee shop.

I began a career working for myself and on my own time without knowing what the future held. Little did I know, I would be starting to write a book a few months later.

I won't be the first one to tell you that the unknown adds a significant amount of stress onto people. Maybe due to my history of investing in the market, I was more comfortable with it. Maybe, it was because my Dad had worked for himself for twenty years, and he always seemed to find a way.

I was lucky enough to have a relationship with a small-but-growing emergency management training and consulting company back in Denver, where I grew up. The company was founded by my Uncle Todd, and at the time, I was a part-time MBA student at Georgetown. When I asked him if there was anything I could do for his company, he asked me,

"What can you bring to the table?"

I desperately went through all of my course materials, trying to figure out what value or experience I could bring to a company in an industry I knew nothing about. I found the final study deck from my marketing class and applied each principle in it to his firm.

"How about this?" I asked.

"You're hired."

That first client may be the most important you ever have. Most likely, they will come from your network, either professional or personal.

Having one client locked down before starting on your own is extremely important, but it is not always possible. So, as I continued to learn more about being an independent worker, I found that I was joining a movement of sorts.

The working relationship we have with employers was and still is changing rapidly.

There were already fifty-seven million Americans who freelanced in 2019, and that was before a single soul got laid off due to coronavirus and the resulting recession.[1] I wanted to explore more about these people and learn how I could be successful on my own.

To me, the best way to learn how to be a free agent is to listen to the stories of those who've done it before me and understand their mindsets before and during their time on their own.

---

1   "Freelancing in America: 2019," Upwork/Freelancers Union, LinkedIn SlideShare, September 23, 2019.

You might be thinking that reading a book about being self-employed is going to be overwhelming. The idea of being on your own is scary, right? That doesn't have to be the case, and you'll see that a lot of people in this book are not big risk-takers; rather, they are people who are very calculated, many of them planning for years before jumping in.

While this is not a "how-to" book, I will present some themes in this book about what the different free agents I heard from did to be successful. You may have heard people talk about the future of work, like it's in some far-off land that we will someday arrive at. It's on its way, and free agents are set up to thrive, if prevailing factors let them.

You will see why freelancing or independent contracting is something you should consider now, or at least something that needs to be in the back of your mind. If you aren't ready to go out on your own at this time, these lessons are applicable to corporate careers as well. The future of work may look significantly different from the way we work now, and you don't want to be caught off guard.

Free agency as I'll call it, is as much about mental preparation as it is a financial one. The new lifestyle brings so much uncertainty about what's to come and how to measure personal risks.

Questions you most likely will have to answer at some point include:

- What am I going to do?
- How do I get started?
- How am I going to get clients?

These types of questions keep people from making the change they know they are ready for. My advice: don't let that be you.

Expectations are that by 2030, over half of the United States will be freelancers.[2]

Are you ready?

---

2   "Freelancing in America: 2017," *Upwork/Freelancers Union,* LinkedIn SlideShare, September 2017.

PART 1

THE FUTURE OF WORK

CHAPTER 1

RISK & THE GIG ECONOMY

———

"The way that companies employ office workers today is outdated and 'insane.'"

— PATRICK PETTITI, CO-CEO OF
CATALENT TECHNOLOGIES[3]

Did you know that in 2017, thirty-nine percent of heterosexual couples met online?[4]

---

3   Michael Selby-Green, "The Gig Economy Is Coming for Your Office Job - Here's How It Works for Companies Doing It Already," *Business Insider,* May 28, 2018.

4   Michael J Rosenfeld, Reuben J Thomas, and Sonia Hausen, "Disintermediating Your Friends: How Online Dating in the United States Displaces Other Ways of Meeting," *Proceedings of the National Academy of Sciences,* August 20, 2019, pp. 17753-17758.

While it may not be considered the most romantic way to meet the love of your life, for many, it's the most effective.

Algorithms already match you with everything else in your life, whether it's Netflix telling you what movie to watch or Amazon telling you what product to buy, why not let a company tell you whom to date?

Much like a dating app, Catalent runs a matchmaking service, only instead of finding your next date, the app is finding you your next project to work on. A company posts a job describing the scope of the project and the skills needed, then the service uses an algorithm that matches them to you and your smiling headshot.

What kind of person is going to set up an entire profile, put in multiple applications, and wait to get matched for a project? And why would they do this when they had the opportunity to be in a stable full-time job?

Welcome to the gig economy.

The Merriam-Webster dictionary describes the so-called "gig economy" as "economic activity that involves the use of temporary or freelance workers to perform jobs typically in the service sector."[5]

In other words, it's the replacement of full-time traditional labor with temporary or on-demand workers.

---

5   *Merriam-Webster.com Dictionary*, s.v. "gig economy," accessed June 6, 2020.

Freelancing has become one of the largest and fastest-growing types of employment in the United States, with fifty-seven million, or thirty-five percent of Americans having freelanced in 2019.[6] The share of full-time freelancers increased eleven percent over the five years between 2014 and 2019.[7]

Companies like it as a way to increase the flexibility they have with their payroll and to save on overhead costs such as healthcare and training.

Even Google, the company that created the "ideal" work environment for its employees, complete with free childcare, free lunch, and a free shuttle to work, has more contractors than actual employees.[8]

So, we know there are a lot of people included in this so-called "gig economy," but with so many terms out there, I wanted to define some that will come up within the book.

- **Free Agent:** The umbrella title covering every sub-category besides gig worker and entrepreneur listed below. When I say free agent, I want you to think of someone who has a skill that would historically be a full-time job, only a free agent works for themselves. "Independent worker" or "self-employed person" would be other terms

---

6   Upwork/Freelancers Union. "Freelancing in America: 2019," LinkedIn SlideShare, September 23, 2019.

7   Ibid.

8   Johan Moreno, "Google Follows A Growing Workplace Trend: Hiring More Contractors Than Employees," Forbes, May 31, 2019.

I use. You are responsible for paying yourself, your taxes, your healthcare, and saving for retirement.

- **Freelancer**: The majority of the people I've interviewed in this book fall under this category. Freelancing means working on a project by project basis. We often think about them in creative fields such as graphic designers, photographers, and writers. They are paid for the project and don't have a long-term contract with a company. They receive 1099 tax forms from the companies that they receive revenue from. Many freelancers will have multiple contracts going on at one time.

- **Independent Contractor:** There will be a significant amount of overlap between contractors and freelancers. Contractors typically have longer-term contracts with companies but receive 1099's and file taxes the same way as freelancers.

- **Solopreneur:** A newer term that was coined only a few years ago. A solopreneur sets out to start a business by themselves without the intent of hiring any other employees. What separates a solopreneur from a freelancer is the goal of how they create their income. Solopreneurs are looking to have their businesses make money while they are golfing or sleeping and may hire subcontractors to do work for them, whereas freelancers only make money while they are working on or completing a project.

- **Gig Worker**: For this book, gig work involves short term contracts between a worker and the customer, usually with a company acting as an intermediary. The people that rely on an app to provide the work for them and are working in a field that would not be considered "skilled" fall into this category." Think of gig workers as drivers for car-sharing companies such as Uber or Lyft.

- **Entrepreneur**: A pure entrepreneur intends to grow and scale their company, hire individuals, and create a traditional full-time job for themselves. I'm including entrepreneurs in this list to help you understand the differences between the types of free agents while admitting that we won't be covering entrepreneurship with much detail in this book. However, many entrepreneurs do start as free agents with no plan for the growth they end up seeing.

FUTURE OF WORK

Is the gig economy good or bad for workers? It's a fair question, and the answer depends on whom you ask. Your opinion is going to depend on how much importance you give to flexibility.

A McKinsey study done in 2016 shows that forty percent of the independent workforce, or twenty-seven million Americans, are "casual earners" and use the gig economy as a way to supplement their income without a clear financial need to do so.[9] They typically will have a full-time job and supplement their income by driving for Uber or renting out their house on Airbnb.

While these casual earners are an important part of the gig economy, for this book, our focus will be on freelancers, solopreneurs, and independent contractors who work "skilled" jobs by themselves. These three all have similar situations

---

9   James Manyika et al., "Independent Work: Choice, Necessity, and the Gig Economy," McKinsey & Company, October 2016.

and issues that other gig workers or entrepreneurs may not completely relate to.

If you're wondering whether the free agent lifestyle is all it's cracked up to be, just note that fifty-one percent of freelancers interviewed in 2018, said that no amount of money would entice them to switch back to traditional employment.[10]

What is it about working on your own that leads people not to seek traditional jobs that could potentially pay them more and, you'd expect, bring them more security? How much value do they place on flexibility and, most importantly, how are they able to be successful? Many of these questions can only be answered by you, but we're going to share some insight into what it's like to be a free agent.

The topic of being a free agent will likely only continue its increase in its importance over the next few years. Forty percent of moonlighters or part-time freelancers have considered leaving their primary job to become completely independent.[11] That's another 5.9 million Americans who already are thinking about becoming self-employed.[12]

---

10 "Freelancing in America: 2019," Upwork/Freelancers Union, LinkedIn SlideShare, September 23, 2019

11 "Freelancing in America: 2019," Upwork/Freelancers Union, LinkedIn SlideShare, September 23, 2019

12 Ibid.

UNCERTAINTY

You might now be saying, "It's not for me. It's way too difficult to pull off and between my family, my student loans, and the sheer humiliation I'll feel once I fail, it's just too risky."

It's no secret that people like certainty in their life. That's why they admire entrepreneurs from afar and watch movies and read books about those who lived in the face of uncertainty.

In his book, *Thinking Fast and Slow*,[13] Nobel Prize in Economics-winning psychologist, Daniel Kahneman discusses the research he and his former research partner Amos Tversky labeled "prospect theory" back in 1979. Prospect theory dives into why people make decisions that are seemingly against the odds because of their inclination to go with what is certain.

Let's see this in action:

If I were to tell you that you have two options, which would you choose?

Option 1: One-hundred percent chance of winning $900.[14]
Option 2: Ninety percent chance of winning $1,000 and a ten percent chance of coming out even (no gain, no loss).

Most rational people would take the sure thing of winning $900. The extra $100 in this scenario just isn't worth the risk.

---

13   Daniel Kahneman, *Thinking, Fast and Slow* (New York: Farrar, Straus and Giroux, 2013), 280.

14   Ibid.

What if we flip that around and these are your two options?

Option 1: One-hundred percent chance of losing $900
Option 2: Ninety percent chance of losing $1,000 and a ten percent chance of coming out even.

For most people, the natural inclination is to take on more risk than the previous scenario because the ten percent chance now looks a heck of a lot better than it did previously.[15] If it's between taking a loss and netting zero, people's aversion to risk seems to dissipate, and they are willing to take their chances even though the odds are against them.

There are three elements that Kahneman and Tversky found that goes into prospect theory, all of which can be applied to the thought process of a free agent.

Certainty: People tend to prefer options that are certain over options that carry risk.[16] It's the same reason there is a higher percentage of millennials invested in a conservatively allocated portfolio (forty-two percent) than there are Generation X (thirty-eight percent) or baby boomers (twenty-three percent).[17]

15   Aurora Harley, "Prospect Theory and Loss Aversion: How Users Make Decisions," *Nielsen Norman Group*, June 19, 2016.

16   Ibid.

17   Andrea Coombes, "Millennials Are Good at Saving, But Investing? Not So Much." *Forbes*, March 13, 2018.

Although millennials have already seen a couple of market crashes in their adult years, it comes back to choosing the most certain option, even though they have less to lose. This type of investment behavior may end up costing a significant amount of future value for the individuals.

It's a similar situation when you think of being self-employed. At the end of the day, people like knowing what their paycheck is going to look like every month and even if being a free agent gives you more freedom, more control, and maybe even a higher salary, the risk of not knowing is a risk that not all are willing to take.

Framing/Isolation Effect: When given multiple options, people tend to ignore the similarities and focus on the differences.

Between quitting your job or being laid off, which would make you more likely to become a free agent?

In reality, both scenarios put you in the same position. You are out of a job and are now deciding if this is the right time to go out on your own. However, I'm sure most of you would point out that there is a difference between being laid off and quitting on your own. After being laid off, do you suddenly feel that you have less to lose and are willing to take on risks that you wouldn't have previously? That would be the isolation effect.

Loss Aversion: This is the whole "I hate losing more than I like winning" mantra that is supposed to define athletes. The excitement of winning doesn't always match up to the disappointment in losing. Instead, people's fear of losing may cost them their chance at winning.

For a free agent, this can be seen in multiple ways. The thought of missing out on a project or negotiating a contract may feel a little overwhelming. After all, what happens if you press too much on pay and lose the opportunity for the contract?

The opportunity cost of going out on your own is certainly a consideration as well. If you were to quit your job tomorrow, you may not only have months of salary you stand to lose. You may also have the benefits that your employer provides, the friends you have at the office, and even the reputation you've built up within the company.

Is that too much to risk?

Maybe, but in 2018, sixty-five percent of full-time freelancers say that having a diversified portfolio of income from multiple clients is more secure than having one employer. The perception of freelancing as being a more secure job was up twelve percent from the 2016 survey.[18]

---

18 "Freelancing in America: 2019," Upwork/Freelancers Union, LinkedIn SlideShare, September 23, 2019

As the dust settles from COVID-19, are you sure your job is as safe as you thought it was?

SLOW AND STEADY

Going out on your own doesn't have to be an incredibly risky option. So, to put everyone at ease, let me tell you a story about a freelancer who took the slow, more cautious approach to being their own boss.

Jennifer received her undergraduate degree in management information systems through the school of business at George Mason University in Fairfax, Virginia. Upon graduation, she started working on a project for a government contractor doing engineering work. Before she knew it, six and a half years had gone by and her job hadn't changed much at all.

Then, an opportunity came for her to build upon one of the pieces of her job that she enjoyed the most: business development.

In her previous role, she spent a significant amount of her time working on developing proposals for government contracts, but it was only a piece of her job. While she debated whether or not to make a change, her natural curiosity won out and she decided to take on the opportunity.

The opportunity now was for her to work full-time as a proposal manager. It would present many new challenges for her, like leading a software programming team and finding solutions to bring to the government.

After working full-time in that capacity for another couple of years, a friend of hers asked Jennifer to join her in taking a course structured around running a business.

Jennifer obliged and learned from the lawyer running the course all about taxes, company structures, and issues that self-employed individuals need to be cognizant of. The year was 2006, and while she always knew that she wanted to be a self-employed consultant someday, she was not prepared to make the leap and decided to continue building on her skill set.

"For me, what I needed was the confidence to take that step. Knowing that if something complex comes in front of me, am I going to know how to tackle it?" Jennifer shared.

But tackle it she did.

After eight years of tackling the largest, most complex strategic proposals at several top-tier government contractors, she had the confidence to go out on her own. Jennifer turned in her resignation weeks before completing her last proposal, working right up until the end.

That was February of 2014, years after she initially took the course on self-employment. Up until that point, she had been meticulously preparing herself to go on her own.

Her most important task was preparing herself financially for the uncertainty that was to come.

Sounds risky, right?

What differentiates Jennifer from others is that she didn't have clients lined up right away and decided to use that first month for what she described as a "decompression period."

"I wanted to get my business in place, my infrastructure set up, pick a laptop, and figure out what printers and software I was going to need. Then, get all the actual administrative things like a bank account and P.O. box, business licenses, and all of these things in place before going out looking for work."

Staying disciplined and doing everything you set out to do can be very tough, and the preparation Jennifer started with, even years before going out on her own, ultimately led to a very successful transition into the freelance world.

Serial entrepreneur, investor, and owner of the NBA's Dallas Mavericks, Mark Cuban agrees, saying, "taking that first step is always the hardest. It's terrifying, but it's about preparation."[19]

So how about that first client?

"In my field, there are consulting companies that will go out and find independent people and match them up with clients," Jennifer began telling me.

She expected the majority of her work to come from these companies and set out to put some agreements in place. She never counted on the fact that people would be reaching out to her directly.

---

19 Ryan Robinson. "60 Entrepreneurs Share Best Business Advice & Success Tips," RyRob.com (blog), February 6, 2020.

Within just a few weeks, Jennifer's idea of her business model had completely changed before her eyes. Instead of relying on these consulting companies, she now was receiving seventy percent of her revenue in the first year from her professional network.

"It's now years later and I could not have more appreciation for the value of the network of people that I had built up over the last ten years of working at various companies,"

When I asked Jennifer about what qualities make a good freelancer, she gave me three very easy-to-understand concepts, which apply to all businesspersons.

- Be a problem solver
- Be naturally curious
- Be authentic

Notice that her list does not include "risk-taker."

I realize that everyone may not be in Jennifer's shoes. She had years of experience and took her time before transitioning into a free agent capacity. Some of you may have lost your job or are only a few years out of college.

Later in this book, I will introduce you to others who faced similar dilemmas, but when deciding whether being a free agent is right to you, start with this question:

"What do I have to gain?"

After assessing what winning would look like for you, with as little emotion as possible, ask yourself this question:

"What do I have to lose?"

In the next chapter, we'll dive right into the opportunities out there for free agents and what "winning" has looked like for them.

CHAPTER 2

THE OPPORTUNITY

―――

"It's the riskiest time in human
history to play it safe."

― CHASE JARVIS, PHOTOGRAPHER, ENTREPRENEUR
AND FOUNDER OF CREATIVELIVE20

It's a chilly, spring day in the nation's capital, only a few months after the market crashed in October of 2008. The country is in crisis, millions of people are getting laid off, and millions of homes are foreclosing. They are calling it the "great recession."

It sounds like an ideal time to start a business, right?

Well, that's what Vanessa saw.

―――――

20 Chase Jarvis, "How to Find Your Creative Calling," interview by Kevin Rose, *The Kevin Rose Show,* Podcast Notes, September 22, 2019

At the start of the recession, Vanessa had gone back to school to finish up her master's degree. Before her return to school, she had been an event planner at a large, worldwide organization and took her experience to an internship where she was only receiving credit.

The outlook for a career in event planning was looking bleak in the short term. Left and right, Vanessa saw many jobs in the events, communication, and marketing sector being some of the hardest hit. Within a blink of an eye, paying someone a decent salary to plan events was no longer feasible.

One day, while sitting in class, the professor asked everyone to create a business plan for a public relations firm. During the process, she made connections in her mind and thought about possible business models that could be transferable to event planning.

The project created an enticing proposition for her. She knew the job market was going to be tough and that everyone who had an internship wanted to turn it into a full-time job. She also knew that companies had smaller budgets for these positions, and full-time employment was a significant cost for them.

So, she did it. She went out on her own.

"But you need job security," Vanessa's mom shared with her daughter.

After all, we did just say how the number of jobs in events was decreasing.

Vanessa took her turn into self-employment by finishing her internship and coming on as a contractor to complete an event. She had her first client.

Upon hearing she was taking on contract work, the organization she worked for before she left for her master's degree reached out asking her for help. They needed her only for two days a week, giving Vanessa income she could count on while giving her time to go out and promote her business.

Reminiscing about her initial start, Vanessa shared with me that there was no job security at the time. "With what I did for a living, the fact that many were getting fired from their full-time job, some would get fired then rehired as a consultant, and this was a great way to get started."

In Washington, D.C., associations, nonprofits, and other organizations host their significant annual events and galas to fund much of their revenues for the year. Vanessa knew this before going in. Her understanding of the market she served in allowed her to feel confident in her decision.

"I just came in at an opportune time."

To start her own company in the worst job situation of her life is a bold move, and her mindset played a large part.

Being a successful freelancer is about finding a space within a market where your skills and abilities are appreciated and of use.

Vanessa, knowing that money was tight for most organizations, was perfectly willing to take smaller contracts than her competitors, allowing her to get started and having a sufficient number of clients right away. The organizations took solace that she was not scheming for a full-time job. That knowledge made it easy to bring her on, and then back again when more help was needed.

Her philosophy has been that she can work quicker and more efficiently than her competitors. She created a differentiation that she used to separate herself from the rest of the industry. It led her to continuously charge more and build a strong reputation.

Vanessa shows how entrepreneurial freelancing can be, and just like any business book would tell you, it's about looking for opportunities and taking advantage of them when they are right in front of you.

After a decade of event planning, she still operates on her own and has built a community around her that she can rely on to help promote her work. Rather than going to networking events for event and hospitality industries, Vanessa started going to tech, science, political, and other industry networking events.

Instead of being in a room with hundreds of other event planners competing for the same business, she was in a place with hundreds of wealthy people who knew nothing about planning large scale events. But they still had launch parties, grand openings, fundraisers, or campaign events that needed planning. This strategy was her diamond-in-the-rough concept that saved her time, energy, and almost always guaranteed more leads.

Vanessa's story gives us a great insight into the mindset of and the opportunities for free agents. Her acceptance of perceived risk created a lane for her that others in her field may have been unwilling to take. She jumped right in, considered what she could do to build up her business and built a reputation along the way.

In reality, there are two ways to enter this free agent work arrangement: intentionally or unintentionally.

Vanessa chose the intentional path, knowing the economy was grim and the job market was thin. Unfortunately, situations come up where that's the case. With tens of million people filing for unemployment in the wake of COVID-19, many people are having to turn to gig work to try to survive. They become freelancers to try and "get by" while also continuing their search for full-time work. It'll be fascinating to see how many of those millions of people choose to stay as a free agent once the economy has settled again.

While the unintentional change is a meaningful discussion, for this book, we will mostly focus on those who had other opportunities and yet still chose to be free agents on a full-time basis. They had enough with their full-time job (or didn't have one in Vanessa's case) and made a strategic decision to quit and go out on their own. It's where I'd hope most of the readers of this book would be.

Whether it's taking a slow path like Jennifer did in the previous chapter or it's starting with a part-time gig, you can't begin until you try. To know what to strive for, you have to know what's out there for you.

Vanessa shows that not all opportunities look the same, and even in desperate times, we can still find a place as a free agent. Let's take a look at the arrangement of the workforce and where free agents are finding their place within it.

THE CHANGING WORKFORCE

Workforce planning – an organizational process to proactively plan for the talent an organization will need – is seeing younger generations (millennials and Generation Z) plan for the future workforce more so than their older counterparts.[21]

Younger generation managers are three times more likely than boomers to believe that future workforce planning is a top priority in their departments, and over a third of them describe their freelance relationships as ongoing partnerships. [22,23] They are leading organizations by using more free agents to maximize their human capital resources.

Using freelancers and contractors instead of full-time employees not only allows for organizations to save money

---

21   Staff Report, "Why You Need Workforce Planning," workforce.com, October 24, 2002.

22   "Future Workforce 2019: How Younger Generations Are Reshaping the Future," *Upwork/Inavero*, LinkedIn SlideShare. March 5, 2019.

23   Ibid.

on overhead expenses, but it keeps them from having to do costly and disappointing layoffs after a major contract or project is over. For managers that can see when gaps in coverage are coming, the ease of hiring independent workers will become invaluable.

This type of activity will only increase as younger generations become managers and decision-makers. Estimates are showing that by 2028 "flexible" talent will comprise twenty-four percent more of department headcount compared to today.[24]

Let's take a look at this in action.

Using highly skilled – typically meaning highly educated – freelancers to connect the gaps in projects can be the best of both worlds for the company and the independent worker.

Let's say you have a new product launch coming, and at the last minute, you realize a shortage of labor in one of the areas. A typical hiring process may take a week to get the job posted, a month of accepting applications, then another two months of interviews, and by the time you hire someone, it's been three months.

Using freelance workers makes sense and seventy-nine percent of executives agree that an on-demand workforce is a competitive advantage.[25]

---

24 Ibid.

25 "The White-Collar Gig Economy," Mavenlink, accessed on May 14, 2020.

It's important to note the difference between highly skilled and highly experienced. If you were a CEO aiming to design your business around the use of free agents, you'd probably think that finding very skillful people to perform specific tasks would be the natural place to start.

However, if you think the only way to become a free agent is to have some sort of individualized skill that you can complete tasks for an organization with, you'd be surprised to find out that it's not true.

Forty-seven percent of executives are looking to fill management and senior executive roles by hiring contractors.[26] Of course, you have to bring a specific set of skills and experiences to those organizations, but it shows that you don't have to give up your free agent lifestyle to work for a company at a high level.

The reason why this book is called "The Free Agent *Mindset*" is that it's doubtful (not impossible) that anyone reading this book will spend their entire career working for themselves. Upon graduating from college, most students don't have any experience that could lead to an independent job that's not driving for Uber.

Having a free agent mindset can start with you while you are younger in your career, but self-employment may not come until later, maybe much later. The two most essential criteria for businesses to have for hiring contractors are specialized degrees (thirty-five percent) and ten or more years of

---

26 Ibid.

experience (twenty-nine percent), followed by coming from a reputable firm (twenty-two percent), and having worked with someone you know (fourteen percent).[27]

While having years of experience is excellent, it's not something all of us have right away. Therefore, having the right mindset when laying out our career may be the most critical.

Free agents have to continually search for those "stamps of approval" along the way to prove their skills and reputation. It can be larger and more expensive stamps that come from universities and degree types, or smaller ones for being certified in a specific skill.

If we were to look at a prototypical M.B.A., they spend a few years after getting their undergraduate degree working in one field, then make the switch to go to business school. After graduation, they hopefully will land a high paying job at a premier management consulting firm or investment bank. At least that's the plan.

During their time in school, they'll take on countless projects, internships, and extracurriculars to bring them new skills. The current mindset would look something like, "I'm working on these projects to help increase my chances of employment at McKinsey or Goldman Sachs." A free agent mindset would change it to, "I'm completing projects to help increase my skill set and develop myself as a business," and could give you a leg up to become self-employed.

---

27 Ibid.

It doesn't mean you shouldn't take a full-time job to build up your skills and leverage it for your career later. Bouncing in and out of self-employment is a stellar way to build experience and qualifications while understanding what purpose every job serves for your professional growth.

Besides, there are going to be times in a person's life when being a free agent may not be as feasible, like when you are attempting to purchase a home or start a family. The firms you then work for as a traditional employee are, in essence, giving you their stamps of approval.

If jumping for high paying jobs isn't your style, and you desire to work for more than just a paycheck, being a free agent may be a natural fit for you as well.

Eighty-five percent of the S&P 500 is now filing sustainability reports.[28] Corporations are beginning to engage in corporate responsibility, and investors are beginning to analyze companies with environmental, social, and governance (ESG) in mind. Unfortunately, the supply of corporate responsibility jobs is low, and it's leaving many people on the sidelines of social responsibility work.

Taking your skills and being independent may give you an advantage to land gigs in this space.

Along with that, what if the way your life is structured gives you little opportunity for a career? Forty six percent

---

28   Susan McPherson, "Corporate Responsibility: What to Expect In 2019," *Forbes*, January 16, 2019.

of freelancers say that freelancing gives them the flexibility they need because they aren't able to work for a traditional employer.[29] What does that look like in action?

THE LACK OF OPPORTUNITY

Holly had a career.

She was the first person in her family to go to college, and while she was there, she met her future husband. He was in the Air Force, and she felt that she now had a partner in life.

Upon graduating, she began her career in corporate communications at a large engineering firm. Holly specialized in creating communication for employees across the country and internationally.

She was good at it, but never loved it.

Just like seventy-six percent of job seekers, Holly realized her boss was toxic and that she didn't like having to report to anyone.[30]

Then an opportunity came for her husband to move to England. Given her situation, it didn't take much thought to ship across the Atlantic Ocean and start their new lives as ex-pats living in England.

---

29 "Freelancing in America: 2019," *Upwork/Freelancers Union*, LinkedIn SlideShare (September 23, 2019).

30 Gene Marks, "Monster Poll: 76 Percent of Job Seekers Say Their Boss Is 'Toxic'," *Inc*, October 18, 2018.

Founder of Expat Child – a website dedicated to helping families adjust in new countries, Carole Hallett Mobbs offers some advice for those who find themselves in Holly's shoes.

"Will you accept that role of 'trailing spouse' and allow it to become problematic for you, or will you grab life by the proverbials and start living it?"[31]

And that's just what Holly set out to do.

Military bases try to support these trailing spouses, but they are typically in smaller towns and filled with people in the same situation. It makes it difficult for these spouses to find employment up to their qualifications.

Because of their typical education levels, military spouses lose out on $12,374 every year from what they are expected to make.[32]

After twenty years, that adds up to almost $190,000 (counting interest) that spouses of our beloved servicemen and women are losing out on!

Holly was in this situation. She bounced around mostly part-time jobs, and during her time in England, she even received her master's degree while working for a university outreach program. Then it came time to move back to the States.

---

31   Carole Hallett Mobbs, "The Trailing Spouse and Identity." *Expat Child (blog),* January 4, 2017.

32   The Council of Economic Advisors, "Military Spouses in the Labor Market," whitehouse.gov, The White House, May 2018.

She and her husband moved to a North Carolina town that was most famous for their Butterball Turkey factory and hours away from a city where her skills would be valued appropriately.

Holly took a job working for the town government, telling me, "it was entry-level bullshit that was terrible."

After taking three and a half years off of traditional work, it was difficult for her to find the right job that matched her skills and experience. She had to continue moving laterally while trying to get any type of job she could.

Talking to other trailing spouses wasn't helpful either. Many of them had found jobs through their technical certificate and were able to perform tasks that didn't require any communication.

Her background was communication, and that was a problem.

"My job relies on relationships, and creativity, and planning, and all these things that you can't certify," she continued.

Without knowing this call would change her working life, Holly talked to a friend one day, expressing her difficulties with finding work. Her friend's family happened to own a small business in Wisconsin that sold waterbeds for dairy cows. By the end of the call, she had asked Holly to come on board as the freelance marketing director.

"I said, 'okay.'"

At that moment, Holly became a freelancer.

Almost one in five freelancers site family obligations as one reason they can't work a traditional job and choose to freelance instead.[33]

Similar to Holly, one of the most heavily impacted families in this situation is military families. When one spouse moves overseas for work, it often is positive and the result of a promotion. The other person in the relationship does not usually see the same benefit and becomes a "trailing spouse."

These aren't just homemakers, either.

A 2018 study from the White House shows us a few interesting facts about Military Spouses abroad. First, forty percent of them have a college degree – that's over ten percent more than the general population.[34]

Another thirty-five percent have some college, once again, well over the general population.[35]

Holly's story shows us that there is no traditional free agent. Organizations seek out freelancers because they fill a need and bring skills that the company either doesn't need or want

---

33 "Freelancing in America: 2019," *Upwork/Freelancers Union*, LinkedIn SlideShare (September 23, 2019).

34 The Council of Economic Advisors. "Military Spouses in the Labor Market."

35 Ibid.

for a full-time employee or only think they need for a short amount of time.

Opportunities are out there for free agents, but you have to be open minded and on the lookout for them. The good news for those looking to be a free agent is that changes are coming, making it much more likely that an opportunity will present itself shortly.

CHAPTER 3

TECHNOLOGY & THE CHANGING WORKPLACE

———

"Computers are useless, they can only give you answers."

– PABLO PICASSO

When, where, and how to work is what defines free agents in the modern world.

Technology is what allows that to happen and is setting out to overhaul business models and completely disrupt how businesses currently operate. Work is changing quickly, and it's impossible to know what employment precisely will look like in ten years.

But we can try to predict it.

While the unknown can certainly be frightening, the natural flexibility that free agents bring should set themselves up for success in the future of work.

The ability for people to communicate and share information when they aren't in the same office has changed the game forever. We've seen many companies slowly adapt overtime to a remote work structure while not wanting to completely go all in, yet.

One potentially positive fallout from COVID-19 is many companies have built remote working abilities, practically overnight. Facebook CEO Mark Zuckerberg has said that fifty percent of Facebook's workforce could be working remotely in the next five to ten years.[36]

While being a remote worker does not necessarily mean you are a free agent, seventy-three percent of all skilled freelancers work remotely.[37] Companies may also become more likely to accept flexible work arrangements as they begin to be more accepting of where employees work —especially considering that almost seventy percent of freelancers say that professionals who are the top in their industry are increasingly choosing to work independently.[38] If that trend continues and a significant proportion of the top talent in the world becomes

36   Riley De León, "Coronavirus Reopening: How Companies Including Facebook, Tesla and Mastercard Are Bringing Workers Back," *CNBC*, May 26, 2020.

37   "Freelancing in America: 2019," *Upwork/Freelancers Union*, LinkedIn SlideShare, September 23, 2019.

38   Ibid.

independent, companies will have to be more accepting of a flexible work arrangement.

Sometimes leaders just need something to spur them in that direction.

COVID-19 may have been the jump starter that was needed to move along remote working trends that had already begun. Tech workers who are tired of paying rents in San Francisco, Seattle, and Los Angeles are moving to lower-cost areas such as Reno, Las Vegas, and Boise, with Boise now seeing 1.57 newcomers for every one person that leaves.[39]

Many of these remote workers stayed with the same companies at a similar salary that they initially had. As many people have now found out during the coronavirus pandemic, working from home isn't too bad — even with the unusual circumstances of having kids and spouses also there with you.

There is a common misconception that it is easy to get distracted by household chores and that your focus will be elsewhere when working from home. It's a reason why some managers have been reluctant to allow remote workers, even though the technology is there.

However, the average telecommuter worked 1.4 more days a month than their traditional counterparts and lost ten

---

39   Ben Eisen, "Workers Are Fleeing Big Cities for Smaller Ones-and Taking Their Jobs with Them," *The Wall Street Journal*, September 7, 2019.

minutes less a day due to distractions.[40] Turns out water coolers and bosses "checking in" are more of a distraction than walking the dog and cleaning the kitchen.

On top of that, when your office is your home or the coffee shop nearby, that twenty-six-minute commute that the average American takes every day turns directly into time that you get to have back.[41]

As more and more companies become comfortable with remote work, it doesn't seem to be that far of a stretch that they would be more keen to hire on-demand workers. For many jobs, if you aren't in the office anymore, do you have to work for the company officially?

But that's just the starting point.

The ease in which companies can now hire you, onboard you, and pay you via online platforms has changed this landscape significantly for both the hiring companies and individuals. Using platforms such as Upwork makes it easy for the freelancer to see the organization's history of paying people on time and look at comments about other's experiences with the firm.

While remote and on-demand work is significant, it's not the subject that's leading the future of work discussion.

---

40   Airtasker, "The Benefits of Working from Home," *Airtasker Blog*, March 31, 2020.

41   US Census Bureau, "Average One-Way Commuting Time by Metropolitan Areas," *The United States Census Bureau*, December 7, 2017.

More changes are coming, and they are putting a lot of traditional jobs at risk and leaving the future of work in question.

THE FOURTH INDUSTRIAL REVOLUTION

Artificial Intelligence (AI) and its destructive nature are coming, and it's bringing its friend, machine learning. McKinsey & Co. estimate that between four hundred and eight hundred million workers globally may be displaced by automation by 2030.[42]

Before we make any decisions for our work situation, let's learn a little bit more about AI and how we can adapt to it.

Artificial Intelligence (AI): the capability of a machine to imitate intelligent human behavior.[43]

Machine Learning: the process by which a computer can improve its performance (as in analyzing image files) by continuously incorporating new data into an existing statistical model.[44]

---

42 James Manyika, Susan Lund, Michael Chui, Jacques Bughin, Jonathan Woetzel, Parul Batra, Ryan Ko, and Saurabh Sanghvi. "Jobs Lost, Jobs Gained: What the Future of Work Will Mean for Jobs, Skills, and Wages." McKinsey & Company, November 2017.

43 *Merriam-Webster.com Dictionary*, s.v. "artificial intelligence," accessed June 2, 2020.

44 *Merriam-Webster.com Dictionary*, s.v. "machine learning," accessed June 2, 2020.

The definitions themselves are a bit unnatural upon first glance, and images of *Terminator* or *I, Robot,* and the robots turning against the humans may be popping up in your mind. But that's the fictional version and not what's happening. Computers are here to make humans' lives easier.

With AI and machine learning, the world is and will continue to have computers do more and more than ever before. Unlike previous advancements in technology, specifically robotics, this technology is not only coming head to head with workers in factories, this one is ready to take on the computer scientists, researchers, and analysts.

Widely considered the father of AI, English mathematician Alan Turing introduced the world to machine learning in 1950. That name may sound familiar to you because Turing was working for the newly created MI6 in World War II, attempting to crack Nazi codes. He was able to break Enigma – the Nazi code deemed unbreakable and ultimately shortened the war.[45]

He died in 1954 at the age of forty-one after being chemically castrated for having a relationship with another man. His war heroics were all but erased even though historians estimate that Alan saved as many as two million lives.

---

45 Chris Smith, Brian McGuire, Ting Huang, and Gary Yang. "The History of Artificial Intelligence." History of Computing. University of Washington, December 2006.

Turing was portrayed by Benedict Cumberbatch in the 2014 Oscar-nominated film, *The Imitation Game*, and has recently become the face of the £50 note.

His published paper in 1950 introduced us to what is now known as the Turing test. He wanted to evaluate whether a computer could imitate human responsiveness. Hence, *The Imitation Game*.

The problem he ran into is the reason AI took a backseat to other forms of technology for the last sixty years: data storage. You can teach a machine "if this happens, do this," thousands of times over, but up until this century, housing that much data was not feasible.

The other area that Turning may have missed on was the ability for machines to learn on their own. He never thought that computers would be able to replicate the learning process of humans, but that is perhaps the most significant area of change to the Turing test.

It turns out that machines definitely can be taught how to learn. As a society, we're finally entering into the stage of machine learning and are only at the beginning of finding out what that means.

Experts are calling this time the fourth industrial revolution, and just like its predecessors, it may completely change the landscape of business as usual. If you need a refresher, let's look at the previous revolutions and quickly discuss their implications.

- **The first revolution** brought the steam engine to the world and wholly altered how humans and information traveled. Its impact was seen highest on textiles as machines could significantly outpace the production of spinning yarn and creating fabric.[46]
- **The second revolution** came around when factories started mass-producing consumer goods, and factories drove workers from small towns into the cities. Before it, most Americans were free agents, and with the factories also came the loss of freedom and independence.[47]
- **The third revolution** began with the computer and the advent of the internet. It forever changed how people communicated and interacted with each other. It also brought forward computer automation processes.[48]
- **The fourth?** That's where we are entering right now. AI and machine learning are leading us to a whole new generation of work.

IMPACT ON BUSINESS

As leaders within organizations try to grapple with the changing workplace, many see the future of companies will be their ability to educate and train their employees rapidly. MIT's *work of the Future* taskforce tells us that when trying to keep up with technology, it's going to be much more than

---

46 History.com Editors, "Industrial Revolution," History.com (A&E Television Networks, October 29, 2009).

47 Eric Niiler, "How the Second Industrial Revolution Changed Americans' Lives," History.com, A&E Television Networks, January 25, 2019.

48 Desoutter Tools, "Industrial Revolution - From Industry 1.0 to Industry 4.0," *Desoutter Tools* (blog), Accessed May 3, 2020.

traditional methods of learning that get our society to where it needs to be. [49]

It's becoming more apparent that learning how to use AI won't be enough, but rather incorporating it as well as machine learning will be a significant layer to the future of education.

While they appreciate the college education they received, over half of all freelancers would replace it entirely with training tailored to their current work.[50] In hindsight, many universities didn't expect this type of arrangement, with ninety-one percent of skilled freelancers wishing that education better prepared them for this way of working.[51]

If this type of work is to take off, how universities and schools are going to adapt their teaching methods to what the workforce needs will become a significant issue in the not so distant future.

If the current education structure won't get it done, companies may decide to create their training systems using AI and machine learning. One thing we do know, education is not going to stop after a bachelor's degree anymore. Solving for how we teach adults will become one of the many challenges the economy faces in the wake of AI.

---

49 "The Work of the Future: Shaping Technology and Institutions," MIT Work of the Future, 2019.

50 "Freelancing in America: 2019," *Upwork/Freelancers Union*, LinkedIn SlideShare, September 23, 2019.

51 Ibid.

We also know that AI is beginning to impact and will continue to change more jobs. It is likely to affect larger metropolitan areas more severely than rural areas and will have a more considerable influence on certain job types over others.[52]

Among the jobs most likely to be negatively affected by AI are ones that typically involve calculating, researching, and analyzing. Such careers as accountants, marketing specialists, and paralegals that are already analytically heavy will be able to deploy machine learning instead of relying on people to analyze the data.[53]

Jobs that will most likely not be negatively impacted by AI include tasks that have extremely human functions like communication, teaching, and motivating. While a computer can predict what movie you want to watch, it's not known for its inspirational speeches.

Many companies and organizations will have to change how their business operates in the upcoming years, and free agents will have to adjust as well. Studies done on the impact AI will have on self-employment are mixed in terms of how positive it is, but all share similar themes. Relationships have staying power.

---

52 Mark Muro, Jacob Whiton, and Robert Maxim, "What Jobs Are Affected by AI? Better-Paid, Better-Educated Workers Face the Most Exposure," *Brookings,* November 20, 2019.

53 Ibid.

Work that cultivates relationships and works well with teams is likely not to see much of a negative impact from AI because it is doing things that AI can't do.[54] You can think of it as a tool in your belt, or your "quant" guy that can run the numbers for you but will be the boss of it. On the other hand, typical independent jobs such as CPAs are going to have a tough time keeping up with advancements in AI if they fail to make changes.

What themes can we take away from what we know about AI?

- Tasks will be gone, consulting and interpreting won't
- Relationships will matter more than ever
- Find ways to incorporate your own AI

An essential element to all of this is that AI completes tasks that currently humans do but won't always have to do.

For example, CPAs will have to look for more ways to provide value when computers complete the majority of their tax preparation services. If they look at themselves more as consultants and relationship builders, they may have more staying power than if they try to compete directly with the computers.

The key to thriving ends up being the ability to excel at your most human capabilities. Can you think critically about problems and provide ideas and solutions that machines

---

54   Kevin Manne, "How Artificial Intelligence Will Impact Self-Employment," *Phys.org*, October 1, 2019.

can't? We were all taught in a rules-based education environment, and the problem is that is how machines precisely learn as well.

But they can't see the big picture; only humans can. Remember, a driverless car will get stuck behind a tree that's fallen over in the middle of a road because it doesn't know how to go around it.[55] You know how to adapt to changing situations, use that to your advantage.

TALENT ANALYTICS

Among trends that have been positive for independent workers is the rise in talent analytics that almost eighty percent of large companies view as urgent or essential.[56] HR leaders are beginning to know exactly what human capital they need and how to measure success from these roles within the organization.

Uses of talent analytics doesn't go back that far. In reality, some of the earliest adopters to measuring human performance using analytics were Major League Baseball general managers.

In Michael Lewis's best-selling book turned movie *Moneyball*, the general manager of the Oakland Athletics, Billy Beane (played by Brad Pitt in the film), began to learn more about

---

55 Matt McFarland, "How Google Is Making Sure Cows Won't Foil Its Self-Driving Cars," *The Washington Post* (WP Company, April 7, 2015).

56 John Houston, and Boy Kester, "Talent Analytics in Practice," *Deloitte Insights*, March 7, 2014.

a man named Bill James and his theories about applying analytics to baseball teams.[57]

After implementing these theories, the Oakland A's would go on to face the New York Yankees in the American League Division Series in 2002. Their payroll was just $41 million, compared to the Yankees which was $125 million.[58] Even though the A's failed to defeat the goliath that was the Yankees, the A's introduced a completely new way of thinking into baseball front offices.

In 2004, the Boston Red Sox used similar analytical models as the A's, while having a bigger budget, and overcame their championship drought and ultimately won the World Series. The successes of those teams helped spearhead the popularity of talent analytics and sabermetrics within baseball.

Analytics allowed Billy Beane to look at historically outcasted players and judge them solely based on their baseball abilities, rather than nuances such as their personal appearance, backgrounds, or other biases. Talent analytics aim to do the same within organizations.

AI and machine learning will only help continue this trend. As organizations implement these technologies and employee analysis, it's likely going to look at many types of jobs that

---

57   Michael Lewis. *Moneyball: The Art of Winning an Unfair Game*, New York, NY, W.W. Norton, 2004.

58   Ryan Wright,"Moneyball: A Look Inside Major League Baseball and the Oakland A's." *Bleacher Report*, September 20, 2011.

are currently considered "safe" and take them away such as your typical mid-level managers.

The administrative tasks that take up so much of a manager's time will all but be gone. Because they will no longer have to manage PTO and other thoughtless tasks, they will get to spend more time doing things that make a good manager, such as coaching, networking, and strategizing.[59] You can foresee a change to a management model of a player-coach, where the manager spends eighty percent of the time working and only twenty percent of their time managing.

Along those lines, AI and analytics will also be used by HR to minimize headcount and maximize efficiencies within the organization.

It's possible that a large firm may realize that it doesn't need one FTE (full-time equivalent) for every job it currently employs right now. In reality, it may need 0.6 or even 0.3 FTE. The company could increase efficiencies by using contract or freelance workers.

The name of the game will become flexibility.

When this happens, already having a free agent mindset and the ability to take your line of work to different industries and companies will put you in a position to succeed.

---

59 Vegard Kolbjørnsrud, Richard Amico, and Robert J. Thomas, "How Artificial Intelligence Will Redefine Management," Harvard Business Review, November 2, 2016.

It's already starting to happen with the popularity of online platforms making it easier to apply for jobs. LinkedIn, Upwork, and many others allow you to have a profile showcasing your skills and efficiently apply for jobs or contracts. Algorithm's then search for the desired qualities specified by the hiring firm. Neither employees nor companies have to go through a long, grueling hiring process anymore.

Overall, using creative new ways to develop hiring processes to find and manage talent will set organizations apart. Creating analytical operating models and using data-driven decision-making practices are going to be the future of work for leadership positions in businesses. All of which will be further on display even more as AI and further technological changes take a stronghold over companies.

There is going to be a lot of change in just a short amount of time. Will you be ready?

CHAPTER 4

GOVERNMENT'S ROLE IN THE FUTURE OF WORK

———

"If the government is covering up knowledge of aliens, they are doing a better job of it than they do anything else."

— STEPHEN HAWKING

Whether we like it or not, the government has a significant role to play in determining the future of work. How they address the impact of AI, machine learning, and changes to the education system will directly impact the types of jobs future generations will work.

On top of the response to technological changes, how the government decides to react to the changing workforce will shape future trends in employment. The more individuals that become free agents, the less government will be able to ignore them. They will have to make real changes to assist these workers in their ventures into self-employment.

Many of the laws and regulations we have around employment were put in place decades ago. Back when the forty-hour workweek became established as the norm, and many workers found themselves in factories.

During WWII, the "Current Tax Payment Act of 1943" was enacted by President Franklin D. Roosevelt and resulted in the W-2 form. This created a "pay taxes as you go" system.[60] Before the act, only four percent of the population made the single annual tax payment they were supposed to make.[61]

Since 1943, there has been only one classification of an employee, and everyone else receives a 1099 – which just shows income received. For free agents, not being considered an employee results in many missed benefits and makes it so some never feel like they can become fully self-employed.

Free agents don't have anyone in their corner fighting for them like traditional employees do. Employees can collectively bargain and benefit from being part of the norm. For freelancers, that'd technically be considered an antitrust violation.

Free agents have very few politicians even thinking about them; however, that could be starting to change. With over half of freelancers being politically active (compared to only thirty-three percent for non-freelancers), independent worker

---

60 "Getting to Know the IRS W-2 Form," American Bar Association, November 27, 2018.

61 Ibid.

needs are going to become some of the more prevalent issues at all levels of government over the next decade.[62]

PORTABLE BENEFITS

In previous generations, getting great benefits was significantly more straightforward than it is today. If you were fortunate enough to get a good job at a decent company, the assumption was that you were set up for life. Unfortunately for most, that's not the reality in today's world. While over eighty percent of people who are retired today receive some sort of pension income, only twenty-four percent of those not yet retired have a defined benefit pension plan.[63]

The switch to 401k's as the prominent retirement plan in this country should have signaled the end to benefits tied to employers. Instead of seeking retirement plans that benefited their employees the most, employers started searching for the lowest-cost program. It's not to say that 401k's are bad products, but why does being a W-2 employee give you the ability to contribute three times more than you can contribute to an IRA (Individual Retirement Account), when they both operate in much of the same ways?

On top of the issues with retirement savings, comes the potentially even more significant aspect of healthcare. Healthcare has become so expensive for many households,

---

62 "Freelancing in America: 2019," *Upwork/Freelancers Union*, LinkedIn SlideShare (September 23, 2019).

63 Lee Barney, "Majority of Today's Retirees Have a Pension," PLANAD-VISER, September 26, 2016.

and they don't even much of a choice in what health plan they pick. Employers have a set few options to choose from, and this limitation continues to hurt workers as around a quarter of employers only allow for high deductible plans.[64]

Many of these benefit plans made sense when most workers would spend much of their career at one company, but the median employee tenure is now only 4.2 years and only 2.8 years for twenty-five to thirty-four-year old's.[65] Opening that many 401k's is inefficient, not just for the employee, but also for the business who has to open them.

The two primary sources of benefits that employees receive from their employers aren't designed for their needs anymore, so what's the solution?

According to a report published by the freelance services marketplace Fiverr, eighty percent of freelancers don't think the government is doing enough to support flexible working with portable benefits.[66]

Portable benefits are a flip from the way the benefit structure in the U.S. is currently. As opposed to receiving your benefits from your employer – which there is no option for a free agent – having portable benefits would allow you to

64 Health Economics, "High Deductible Health Plans: What Are the Pros and Cons?" Knowledge@Wharton, June 17, 2019.

65 U.S. Bureau of Labor Statistics, "Employee Tenure Summary," *U.S. Bureau of Labor Statistics*, U.S. Department of Labor, September 20, 2018.

66 "Research Report: The Freelance Political Perspective Report," *Fiverr*, October 2018.

keep your benefits and have them travel with you to whatever gig you take.

While it is a still-developing market, portable benefits platforms are already starting to pop up. I spoke with Kristen Anderson, founder and CEO of the Boston-based startup, Catch Financial, Inc., to get her thoughts on what's helping or hindering free agents.

"I think there is this massive myth that our system is one that enables choice, rather than what true choice would be, which is that you get to pick the plan that makes sense," Kristen shared.

Over forty million Americans have filed for unemployment in the wake of COVID-19, and many of them either lost their health insurance or now have the burden to pay for it entirely on their shoulders, just when they needed it most.[67]

Most of the talk about portable benefits leads to a government-controlled benefit system, which Kristen believes is a mistake. She told me, "there's a critical role for the private sector, nonprofit and government to work together on this, but the private sector has to be the one who leads the way."

Having the private sector lead the way could look like what Catch has set out to do. It helps independent workers by providing automated tax withholding, health insurance, management of retirement plans, and more to create a more W-2 type feel for free agents.

---

67 Anneken Tappe, "1 In 4 American Workers Have Filed for Unemployment Benefits during the Pandemic," *CNN*, May 28, 2020.

What if the government incentivized companies to contribute to a free agent's retirement accounts as part of their contract? What if you could choose the health insurance that was best for you at a price that was similar to what you would pay as a traditional employee?

Those are some of the questions that the government will need to think about as millions of more workers find themselves working as a free agent.

RESPONSE TO THE GIG ECONOMY

As we talked about in Chapter One, the gig economy is a term that many times doesn't cover what it intends to, yet it's a buzz word in the world right now.

While not encompassing the entirety of the flexible work economy, "gigs" have been around forever. Whether it's cleaning houses, mowing lawns, or walking dogs, people have been working short-term tasks forever. The difference being, twenty years ago, it wasn't possible to go through an app on your phone to have a stranger put together your new Ikea bookshelf.

The apps are where many assume that the gig economy ends, but, in reality, it is only the beginning. The gig economy characterizes the movement but represents many more than just app-based workers. It's the desire to work from anywhere and for any company.

In 2018, eleven major cities had over one hundred thousand skilled independent workers, an eleven percent increase over

2017.[68] These workers had combined revenue growth of seventeen percent while having an eleven percent increase in overall growth, showcasing that being a free agent can pay.[69]

With all of these independent workers out there, you'd expect the government would have taken notice. Remember all of the hoopla around Amazon creating HQ2? That was only over fifty thousand skilled jobs, and some city governments were giving away billions in incentives to try to attract Amazon to their region.[70]

Instead of building brand new office buildings, free agents tend to work from home and do their best to support their local coffee shops and, of course, receive no incentives.

That brings us to the two sides to the gig economy debate; you can view it favorably or unfavorably.

You have one side that loves the flexibility that the gig economy allows for, and another that thinks the business models utilizing flexible work are unfair to workers. Both sides have their merits.

You may have heard that California has been the first and only state so far to try and address the gig economy. It makes sense, as the majority of the gig companies that come to

---

68 "The Independent Workforce: Sizing the Market in the United States," *Fiverr*, 2019.

69 Ibid.

70 Kaya Yurieff. "Everything We Know about Amazon's HQ2 Search." CNN. Cable News Network, November 5, 2018.

mind, such as Uber, Lyft, Postmates, etc., are based out of Silicon Valley. There have also been protests from Uber and Lyft drivers across the country demanding to be treated as regular employees and receive other benefits.[71]

It's clear that California's legislatures responded to the protests, with a lesser focus on how their enacted laws challenge the individuals who craved the flexibility that the gig economy provides.

As it turns out, a large number of Uber drivers and others that take part in the "sharing" economy aren't even treating it as a full-time job. The majority of drivers only last for three months and average about seventeen hours a week.[72]

Most people who are using this section of the gig economy, are using it to supplement their other income or as a temporary fix when they are between jobs. The majority of drivers are not looking to be full-time and adhering to the standards that the law puts in place hurts more than just the tech companies.

It turns out that over eighty percent of full-time freelancers would prefer to take home more pay and purchase the

---

71   Nbc. "Uber, Lyft Driver Protest Brings Manhattan Traffic to Nearly Total Stop at Rush Hour." NBC New York. NBC New York, September 17, 2019.

72   Lawrence Mishel, "Uber and the Labor Market: Uber Drivers' Compensation, Wages, and the Scale of Uber and the Gig Economy," Economic Policy Institute, May 15, 2018.

benefits on their own.[73] The priorities they have for politicians are to make healthcare more affordable and available.[74]

Let's take a look at the three-pronged test that's laid out in the California AB-5 employment law that Uber and Lyft are spending millions to fight right now. To pass the "ABC" test component, the company (not the individual) must prove these three items to label someone as an independent contractor properly:

1. The individual must be free from the company's control.
2. They must perform work that isn't central to the company's business.
3. They must have an independent business in that industry.

Putting Uber and Lyft aside now, let's talk about how this test might influence free agents entering the gig economy.

- Being free from the company's control:

  That shouldn't be too much of an issue. Free agents set their hours, pay themselves, operate on their own. In a lot of ways, it is what free agents care the most about.

- Perform work that isn't central to the company's business:

  Here is where it starts to get murky. It's no secret that many small businesses rely on independent contractors

---

73   "Freelancing in America: 2019," *Upwork/Freelancers Union*, LinkedIn SlideShare (September 23, 2019).

74   IBID

to fill positions that they couldn't afford to pay a full-time employee. Also, when they get an independent contractor, they may be getting someone who has much more experience in a particular area than a full-time employee at a lower wage may have.

What defines work that is central to the company's business, anyways? Considering Uber in 2019 had seventy-six percent of its revenues come from its Rideshare segment, this is California's spot to get Uber. It's a more robust argument to say the drivers aren't central to Uber's business rather than a freelance writer they bring on.

- Independent business in that industry:

Another spot where the law is aiming at Uber, but some free agents will pass. Blog writers may write for multiple places and, therefore, could pass this test. However, not all contract workers can pass this test all of the time. When someone takes on an extended contract, and because of the amount of work needed, it becomes the only contract they have, do they still have an independent business in that industry?

I do not pretend to know every answer to the employment challenges of the gig economy. People love the flexibility they are getting from this future economy, and everyone needs to know the benefits and risks involved if similar laws are proposed in your state.

ATTRACTING WORKERS

This new economy is all about connecting companies and people who can fill their roles quickly. Technology is making this happen and allows these organizations to rethink their methods of hiring, and subsequently, their work models.

Co-founder of AND.CO, a business management software designed for freelancers, solopreneurs, and entrepreneurs, Martin Strutz says that technology "allows companies to tap into specific expertise, bring in outside perspectives, increase the speed to market and engage with the brightest of minds, and not just those nearby."[75] Martin continued, "what is the point in housing thousands of workers, often in some of the most expensive areas of our cities, when communication is mostly done through email, phone or Slack anyways?"[76]

He has an important point.

Why is it that a few coastal cities make up so much of the wealth of the country and leave other once-thriving cities hoping for more?

By the end of the 1970's, per capita income in the St. Louis metro area was ninety percent as high as in the New York

---

75   Martin Strutz, "Freelancers and Technology Are Leading the Workforce Revolution," *Forbes*, November 17, 2016.

76   Ibid.

metro area. In 2018, that number was seventy-three percent and continuing to shrink.[77]

That highlights what many cities across the country are feeling. There are many reasons for these changes, but it's not inconsequential to note that in 1982, guidelines on what constituted antitrust investigations for mergers changed.[78]

The previous consensus, known as the Brandeisian school, was that antitrust policy was there to promote competition, giving the little guys more of a chance.[79] The change came as globalization was taking over, and America wanted to have superior companies again, leading officials to take a laxer position on antitrust and following the line of the Chicago School.[80]

The tide may eventually turn back to the Brandeisian school, which is starting to gain some traction as members from both sides of the aisle are pushing to break up the big companies, especially tech.[81] If these lawmakers get their wish, tech companies will break up in favor of competition and small business.

---

77   U.S. Bureau of Economic Analysis, Per Capita Personal Income in St. Louis, MO-IL (MSA) [STLPCPI], retrieved from FRED, Federal Reserve Bank of St. Louis, May 3, 2020.

78   Phillip Longman, "Why the Economic Fates of America's Cities Diverged," *The Atlantic*, November 28, 2015.

79   Daniel A. Crane, "Antitrust's Unconventional Politics," (2018). *Law & Economics Working Papers*. 153.

80   Ibid.

81   Ibid.

It's not to say that tech companies breaking up would immediately hurt or help free agents. If the big tech companies were to break up, it would most likely be because the government wants to treat the company's platform (like Google's search) as a public utility, forgoing the ability to sell its products on their platform.[82]

Would having smaller companies lead to companies being more innovative with the utilization of their workforce? Would they try to, in essence, share employees? Both of these may help free agents come out from the control of a company but maintain the same level of employment.

Unless these types of changes happen, it's safe to say that headquarters will most likely continue to stay in a few major metropolitan areas for the time being, but that doesn't mean workers are there to stay.

As a way to boost their economy, cities and towns are looking to attract teleworkers by incentivizing them with incredible benefits. Tulsa, OK, for instance, will give you ten thousand dollars, a desk at a downtown coworking space, and other special events if you bring your remote or self-employed job there.[83]

As the remote and independent workforce grows, it will be interesting to see how creative more cities and towns that

82   Herbert Hovenkamp, William Kovacic, and Hemant Bhargava, "Why Breaking Up Big Tech Could Do More Harm Than Good," Knowledge@ Wharton, March 26, 2019.

83   "Tulsa Remote," Tulsa Remote. Accessed May 4, 2020.

haven't had the same economic production as others over the last few decades get. It may work, too.

Free agents want the flexibility to work from wherever, and seven in ten freelancers are open to moving away from large cities if opportunities were the same. Ten percent would even consider being a digital nomad while continuing their business.[84]

The government is going to have a significant impact on the future of work. While this country decides what it means to have a job, innovative cities and towns will have the opportunity to excel by clearing the way for free agents to succeed.

After evaluating what the world looks like for free agents, the obvious next question is, "what would I even do on my own?" Join me for part two, where we will hear from free agents and get ideas of where your place might be in the future economy.

---

84 "Freelancing in America: 2019," *Upwork/Freelancers Union*, LinkedIn SlideShare (September 23, 2019).

PART 2

AGAINST
THE GRAIN

CHAPTER 5

BRING YOUR PASSION, DON'T FOLLOW IT

———

"If passion drives you, let reason hold the reins."

— BENJAMIN FRANKLIN

"Something happened to me, and I became obsessed."[85]

Molly is the subject of the 2017 Aaron Sorkin film, *Molly's Game*. At twenty-two, she was on the U.S. national ski team and competing for a spot on the U.S. Olympic team.

And then she had enough of the pain she'd been dealing with since childhood and decided to retire.[86]

---

85 *Brand Building Through Storytelling*, "Molly Bloom - Poker Entrepreneur – Keynote Speaker - Summit 2018," June 4, 2018.

86 Molly Bloom, *Molly's Game: The True Story of the 26-Year-Old Woman behind the Most Exclusive, High-Stakes Underground Poker Game in the World*, New York, NY, Dey Street Books, 2017.

She moved out to Los Angeles and had no idea what she wanted to do, just that she wanted out of the cold. Eventually, she found an opportunity to start running the poker games that her real estate developer boss hosted in the basement of a bar.

Initially thinking this was another annoying task, it turned out that her boss was a very well-connected man in L.A. As she stood next to the door welcoming the players with her supermarket cheese plate, in walked famous people such as Tobey Maguire and Ben Affleck, among others.

Suddenly her embarrassment hit.

Earlier in the day, she had googled "what kind of music do poker players like to listen to?"[87] Of course, songs such as "The Gambler" by Kenny Rogers showed up, so that's what she played.

Molly watched these poker games and these A-list celebrities playing them with much curiosity. She was determined to understand why they came to this crappy basement bar to play poker when they could be doing anything else in the world. In reality, it was their escape.

So, she saw her opportunity to start running these games herself and to make them bigger. She made the stakes higher, rented out suites at five-star hotels in LA and created a field of scouts that kept their ears open for more players.

---

87 Ibid

It was her opportunity to launch a business completely on her own, and she wasn't going to let anyone take it from her. She began to try to do everything. She was the bank, the bookkeeper, the planner, everything. To keep up with her workload, she started taking drugs, drinking more, and skipping out on the rest of her life. She was obsessed.

At this point, her passion for what she created caused her to look past a lot of questionable activities that she should have noticed. The poker game had moved to New York City and had even wealthier and larger personalities playing in it. The stakes were once again raised, and she was operating as the bank, lending out cash and allowing players to play on credit. Molly was running a full-fledged, high-stake, and barely legal, poker game.

She was just a twenty-six-year-old small-town girl from Loveland, Colorado. Now she was running the biggest poker game in the world.

But then it came crashing down.

Some of these new players had connections to the mob, and the FBI began learning of her games. She had players staking other players (essentially creating a team, A.K.A. cheating) without her noticing, and the whole operation was out of control.

All of her assets were eventually frozen, and she never got them back. She went from being a millionaire to being broke overnight. Finally, she plead guilty to a charge of operating an illegal gambling business and was subsequently sentenced to community service. She then wrote a book that didn't sell well initially and tried to start over.

It's easy to become passionate about what your business is. After all, you're spending forty, fifty, or maybe sixty hours a week on it and sometimes you forget about the world around you. When you're self-employed, you can't let this happen. You are the primary, secondary, and final say of your business, and any surprises (such as bad clients, new technologies, laws, etc.) can kill your business.

You might be thinking that Molly's story is a bit of an exaggeration from what happens to the average person. It's really not that far off. While you may not be hosting underground poker games or doing anything that puts you at risk with the law, passion still can put blinders on us that causes us to overlook things.

Maybe that's forgetting to pay your quarterly taxes, forgetting to set your expectations for a client, or forgetting about your kids Little League game, when we lose track of what's going on around us, it doesn't always end well. It is essential to like what you do, but not to let it control you. Like it *enough*, but don't let it take away from the rest of your life.

PASSION

We've all been told, "do what you love, and you'll never work a day in your life."

It's what the world likes to define as your passion. Today, most job interviewers in one way or another will often ask you, "what gets you out of bed in the morning?" or "what motivates you?"

Corporations like to use passion to describe its mission or its story. For example, Starbucks has listed on its website, "we're not just passionate purveyors of coffee, but everything else that goes with a full and rewarding coffeehouse experience."[88]

I've been to many different Starbucks locations in my life; I will admit that there are certainly some of their employees who exhibit that type of passion and energy for their job.

I've also been to many where passionate is the last word I'd use to describe its employees. How much better of an experience is it when you go to a Starbucks, and you come into contact with one of their passionate employees?

That's the difference between corporations speaking and not the individuals who work at the company. Workers' goals don't always align with the company's goals. You read the company's mission, and you become so excited to visit the store, only to be disappointed by the experience.

U.S corporations know this, and that's why they are spending over $1 billion on employee engagement and over $100 billion on employee training each year.[89]

---

88 "Company Information," Starbucks Coffee Company, accessed May 15, 2020.

89 Deloitte, "Deloitte Study: Only 13 Percent of the US Workforce Is Passionate About Their Jobs," PR Newswire: press release distribution, targeting, monitoring and marketing, June 26, 2018.

Still, only thirteen percent of the U.S. workforce are actually passionate about their jobs.[90] There seems to be a disconnect between the talk about following your passion and actually doing so. Is it because it is difficult to find one's passion, or is following it hard?

A corporation's "passion" is going to be directly in line with the niche and the value they bring to their customers. So, how can companies find or create passionate employees, and does that even matter?

It turns out it does. Seventy-nine percent of adults across multiple countries consider the company's mission before applying.[91] People want to know what the company stands for, what it's doing in the community, and if they are going to be around coworkers with similar values.

Yet, with so many people looking at the mission before applying for a job, you would think that the number of passionate employees would be higher. Maybe passion isn't all that it's cracked up to be when searching for work.

Maybe, the type of work that you are doing matters more than the company's mission statement.

That's where being a free agent really has its perks. Not only do you get to choose when you work and how you work, but you also get to choose what type of work you are doing and

90 Ibid.

91 Team, Glassdoor, "New Survey: Company Mission & Culture Matter More Than Salary: Glassdoor," Glassdoor Blog, July 10, 2019.

for whom you do it. Does that mean you should go right after the jobs you are most passionate about? After all, Molly became so passionate about her career that she lost track of everything else.

Let's see what we can learn from those who have been free agents well before the gig economy was even a thing.

In his eight seasons hosting the show, *Dirty Jobs,* well-known TV actor Mike Rowe learned from the dirty job workers that "only a moron would follow passion; bring it with you, but don't follow it."[92]

Now, you probably didn't grow up dreaming of being a plumber or an electrician, and neither did they. Just like you, they had their eyes set on something more glamorous, something they had more of a desire to do.

That's why we can learn a lot about self-employment from vocational and trade workers. They approached their business not as a passion project but as somewhere they could have a career.

Describing the *Dirty Jobs* approach to being a free agent, Mike said, "first they identified the opportunity, then they got good at it, and then they found a way to love it."

Sounds easier said than done, but if people can turn plumbing into something they love, maybe you can look for

---

92 Mike Rowe, "'Dirty Jobs' Host Mike Rowe: Here's Why You Should Never Follow Your Passion." Interview by Brian Elliot. *Behind the Brand*, Business Insider, December 11, 2014.

something you're actually good at and find ways to make it more interesting.

Professors from Stanford and Yale agree that the "dirty jobs" workers were on to something. The researchers completed a study around the topic of passion and found that setting your sights too much on one interest often restricts you from being open-minded.[93] When you close off your mind, you miss opportunities that are in front of you and can lose track of the real reason you started your business in the first place.

Shutting out the outside world is what ultimately took down Molly. She stopped noticing the world around her because she became so ingrained with her poker games.

If we aren't going to follow our passion, then what should we do as a free agent?

Let's see what we can learn from a wedding photographer.

DO WHAT YOUR GOOD AT

"Honestly, I made it work because I had to make it work."

Morgan is a solopreneur who describes her journey to being self-employed as a necessity rather than a passion. She became a nanny right after high school for a family and did that for years while attending a community college. In her

---

93 Paul A. O'Keefe, Carol S Dweck, and Gregory M Walton, "Implicit Theories of Interest: Finding Your Passion or Developing It?" Psychological Science, 2018.

free time, she enjoyed photography and would occasionally photograph a wedding or an event for money, but she was a nanny first and foremost.

On a spring day, the family she was nannying for told her that they were moving across the country. The timing was not great for Morgan, and amid a lousy job market, she found it difficult to find another job quickly.

Already living on her own, with no one to turn to, she took photography out of her back pocket and decided this was going to be her new career.

In the early days of her photography career, she understandably took everything she could get her hands on.

"I was still new to the industry and didn't really understand even what I was doing," Morgan elaborated while looking back on the early days of her business. "But when you're first starting out, you kind of have to pay your dues a little bit."

After doing a few photoshoots at meager prices, she received some advice from another photographer to raise her rates after every three shoots she did. She was initially worried about the ramifications but quickly found that her rise in prices had no effect on the volume of work she received.

"Photography is not my dream job; it never was."

Morgan never expected to be a photographer for a living, but she also never said no to it. The problem was that she didn't love many types of photography she would get asked to do.

Eventually, a friend of hers asked, "if you had one more session to shoot, what would you want to shoot?"

"I'd photograph a couple."

That's when Morgan realized what she liked most about being a photographer and where she wanted to direct her business. As much as she appreciated the income that came from photographing senior photos, families, and headshots, she ultimately didn't get excited about it.

So how did she start to specialize in what she wanted to do?

It started with her reading a book, titled *Building a Story-Brand* by Donald Miller, that taught her how to brand her business. She learned that a brand wasn't what her logo or Instagram feed looked like; it was what's unique about her business and what the company stood for.

She then turned her focus to building her story around her couples and her as a photographer. She saw the personal connection that wedding couples have with their photographer, and she wanted to make sure they felt as close to her as possible.

That alone is what has caused her business to grow significantly more quickly than it was in the past.

Across all sorts of industries and sizes of companies, Morgan's insights into branding her business can apply. Every self-employed worker wants to grow their business to its full capacity, so how do you take these ideas and choose the clients you want to work with?

"I find that the people who are willing to pay my prices are the people who I absolutely love working with," Morgan said in a seemingly obvious response. We all like clients who pay our price and pay on time, right?

For Morgan and many independent workers out there, prices go deeper than that. Passions and emotions can get in the way of business, and it's what makes being self-employed extremely difficult. When there is no sales-manager to go to, it's easy to hear a client's story and cater your prices to them or be so passionate about their mission that you're willing to accept a lower price.

Sometimes that works out and is very rewarding, but what about when it comes back to bite you?

In Morgan's world of luxury weddings, some couples want to have the most expensive wedding they possibly can have, yet they do not want to pay the photographer, who is supposed to capture the entire essence of the event, what they're worth.

On one of the first weddings that she photographed, a couple had a very extravagant wedding and found Morgan because, at the time, she was very inexpensive. Even still, they pushed Morgan to do it cheaper than even a newer wedding photographer should charge.

Morgan accepted the job and saw red flags early on, but she still pushed through to do the best work she could do at the time. Looking back at the event, she remembered the disappointment the couple shared about the photos and how she did everything she could do to try to make it up to them.

The couple had been unhappy with every vendor in the wedding, most likely suffering from the "post-wedding blues."

"Post-wedding blues" are a phenomenon that many couples see immediately after their wedding day. With all of the excitement and energy surrounding them leading up to the big day, there can be a letdown after it's over. Morgan hadn't been exposed to it yet and didn't know how to react to their criticism.

Those photos may not be the same level of quality that she would take if she were to do them today, but taking in the price the couple received, the photos were a steal.

Morgan learned from that experience that allowing yourself to take a lesser amount than you're worth wasn't going to work out in her favor. She now has a set pricing sheet that every set of couples works off of and has found great success in specializing herself as a luxury wedding photographer.

Morgan's story shows that while you are self-employed, doing what you are good at, not just what you are passionate about, can lead to lots of success. Along those same lines, when we are narrowing our focus of work, it's crucial to have an idea of the clients that you want to work with.

Just like any business, choose a target market that has enough demand for your services and find your position within it. Then, be sure to price your services accordingly.

Both Molly and Morgan took the same approach of building off of what they were good at and then applying it to a niche that they enjoyed. It shows us how we can take a skill of ours and make it a career as a free agent. Even though her initial try at being a free agent turned out poorly for Molly, we can learn just as much as we can from Morgan.

Molly got overwhelmed by her business, and it cost her the life she had created for herself but it started on the right track. She saw an opportunity where her services were needed; she just became too afraid of things running without her. Instead of subcontracting out or saying "no" to the increase in business, Molly turned to drugs to keep her awake. Morgan, on the other hand, noticed she was taking on too much work and found younger and less experienced photographers that she could teach and subcontract some of her work out to.

Passion is a potent tool that needs to go in your belt; it's what motivates you to get up at eight o'clock in the morning when you comfortably could sleep until eleven. However, passion can cause us some trouble if we let it get the best of us.

If you want a job to consume your life, find your passion, but know that it may get the best of you someday. If you're looking to work so you can enjoy life outside of work, maybe create a career that isn't what you would consider your passion but something that comes more naturally to you.

You just may end up happier that way.

CHAPTER 6

BE CREATIVE & THINK DIFFERENTLY

___

"It's more fun to be a pirate than to join the Navy."

– STEVE JOBS

From inventing a coffee table book about coffee tables to selling raincoats and old vinyl records, no one may embody the freedom associated with being a free agent more than the eccentric character in the 1990's sitcom *Seinfeld*, Kramer. The free-spirited neighbor of Jerry never seems to have a job, but he is always up to some scheme and brings Jerry along with him.

I bring up Kramer not because I think any of those reading the book should strive to have a life like the one Michael Richards plays on TV, but rather to discuss the show in which he became famous on. *Seinfeld* was not like other shows at the time. It offered no storyline, there was never a plot, and it took people a little bit to even understand the point – to which was there was no point.

Jerry grew up in a middle-class town in Long Island. As a kid, he realized he was funny when he made one of his friends spit his milk and cookies out because of a joke Jerry made. Making people laugh became Jerry's favorite thing to do. As Jerry grew up, he became obsessed with two things: comedy and cars.[94]

However, Jerry did not look at comedy like everyone else did. He thought of it as more of a science than any others before him had. To him, a good joke was logical and formulaic. The difference is the content and the silly twist at the end.[95]

While in college, Jerry would go down to the comedy clubs and treated his time there as an independent study. He used it to research what worked and what didn't. He even wrote a forty-page paper on the subject of comedy. Depicted during an episode of *Seinfeld*, Jerry was known for having a tape recording during his shows and studying the crowd reactions. His formulaic approach was what ultimately drove his success.

Jerry and his partner, Larry David, would sit at a coffee shop and talk about what the show should be about. Eventually, they concluded that doing just that should be the show;

---

94 Jennifer Keshin Armstrong, *Seinfeldia: How a Show About Nothing Changed Everything,* New York, NY: Simon & Schuster Paperbacks, an imprint of Simon & Schuster, Inc., 2017.

95 Ibid.

sitting around a coffee shop and talking was worthwhile television. You know what? They were right.

Jerry and Larry saw the box of comedy that everyone else had played in before and decided to create their own box. Looking at something a different way is where innovation comes from.

Had he not thought about comedy differently, nothing would have separated him from other comedians, and we would not have been blessed with one of the top shows of the 1990s.

To innovate is to do something in a new way; it's as simple as that. Even though comedy is a creative field, the approach that Jerry took to his craft was not just creative; it was innovative. Jerry innovated by performing a different kind of comedy, creating a different type of TV show, and by using a different sort of approach.

Even if you're not in what's considered a creative field, the need for innovation is there. Everyone's been told to "think outside the box" at some point. Maybe it happened in a team meeting, directly from your upper management or from a teammate on a project.

When we intentionally try to think creatively, we wind up sitting there staring at the walls, tapping our pens mindlessly, and ultimately getting nothing accomplished.

Why is it so hard to intentionally come up with a new idea? For free agents, does innovating even matter?

Yes.

There is a stereotype that most freelancers are in creative fields. When you think of someone describing themselves as a freelancer, the occupations that typically come to mind are journalist, photographer, and maybe graphic designer?

It's not your imagination; seventy-five percent of arts and design workers are freelancers, significantly more than any other occupations.[96] Why is it that creative fields have so many freelancers, but others don't? Is it because companies undervalue original work and don't want to spend their precious budgets on them? Or rather, does being in a creative field make the worker want to be independent?

It's also not to say you have to be in a creative field to freelance. Many other occupations such as construction, sales, and finance each have over thirty percent of their composition coming from freelancers.[97]

Good or bad, being an independent worker separates you from other firms that you may be competing with. To be a successful free agent, you must differentiate yourself from your peers. Otherwise, companies will stick with what they know and continue to hire agencies or other companies.

Initially, your differentiator can be on price. Still, the goal is not to create a business undercutting the competition; that

96 "Freelancing in America: 2019," *Upwork/Freelancers Union*, LinkedIn SlideShare, September 23, 2019.

97 Ibid.

doesn't usually prove to be sustainable, nor beneficial to you and your field. You didn't set out on this path to take home less money than you previously did. The goal should be finding a way to charge more for your services while, at the same time, increasing your value to your clients.

Being solo gives you this distinct advantage.

THINK DIFFERENTLY

Innovating is hard. Creative thinking is also hard. What makes it even more difficult is when you have to foster thirty or more people in a boardroom and have creative discussions. You just can't do it. It's why one of the creators of Pixar, the animation firm behind *Toy Story, Finding Nemo*, and *The Incredibles*, Ed Catmull, wrote a book on attempting to foster creativity.

In his book, *Creativity, Inc.*, Mr. Catmull discusses that Pixar was continually trying to battle with how to best foster creativity in a room full of creative individuals.[98] He knew the odds were stacked against them as most companies run into a wall and have a hard time producing the same quality of work time after time.

Pixar did away with the big conference room tables and nametags and tried to remove all sense of hierarchy in the

---

98   Ed Catmull, and Amy Wallace, *Creativity, Inc.: Overcoming the Unseen Forces That Stand in the Way of True Inspiration*, New York, NY, Random House, 2014, 1.

room. That's not an easy task for a big corporation, but they have many minds working on finding solutions; you have one.

Working alone presents different challenges to creativity other than just removing obstacles. The whole premise of being a free agent is that many of these obstacles are already gone, yet it's still tricky to step back and see things differently. When a company brings you on, you are the one expected to come to the boardroom with ideas.

To learn how to apply a more creative approach to your job, we first need to learn more about what it means to think differently and how to foster it.

In season one of the hit TV series *Mad Men*, fictional creative director extraordinaire Don Draper tells his then receptionist, Peggy, how great ideas come to us. Saying, "Peggy, just think about it deeply, then forget it, and an idea will jump up in your face."[99]

Don was on to something.

There is a process we can follow into creativity that has been studied and studied again. Creativity pioneer Mihaly Csikszentmihalyi, Ph.D., tells us the three steps for creating.[100]

1. **Immersion:** This is the phase when you are completely locked in on your work and have unrelenting focus.

---

99 "Indian Summer," *Mad Men*, USA, October 4, 2007.
100 Linda Naiman, "3 Keys to Finding a Creative Breakthrough," Creativity at Work, October 21, 2019.

2. **Incubation**: The next phase is when rest your brain and are not thinking at all about your work.
3. **Insight**: This happens when you come to a new realization. You've let your mind wander, and, believe it or not, it came up with something.

So, how do we, as an individual, start thinking more creatively and apply it to our craft?

It starts with not trying to create the latest and greatest product, but just taking a step back from your job and trying to look at things differently. We can think outside the box by simply applying a new way of thinking or taking a different approach to our craft.

Let's see these principles in action, though. What does it look like when we as individuals begin to look at their expertise and skills from a different perspective?

Joshua lived in Tucson, A.Z., and grew up with a self-described entrepreneurial mind. He remembered growing up with a father who was a construction worker, and at an early age, he learned how to negotiate. He was eight years old when he first ventured into business, cutting and servicing lawns until he was about fifteen.

Music was always his passion. He dreamed of building his dream recording studio, one that he could run and host artists in.

So, what did he do? He joined the military.

His first station was in England, and because of his new increase in money, he was able to afford everything he needed for his home studio. In an effort to educate himself and learn the latest equipment, he would bring people in to try it out. Over time, he started making a name for himself in the overseas community, and people began paying him to use his studio.

Eventually, Joshua grew tired of the constant negotiations with local artists and shifted his focus to commercial recordings where he saw a more natural way of doing business. At this time, he had been focused on audio for fifteen years of his life and had only briefly tipped his toes into video.

When initially setting up his studios, he had created YouTube videos to showcase what he was building. After a couple of times filming birthday parties for his girlfriend and other friends, he started wondering if there might be an opportunity in video.

Just like he had done in building his studio, he went directly into research mode. In only a few months, he taught himself the tools and techniques he needed to succeed but had one major problem.

Everything he needed was extremely costly.

"I can't keep buying new video equipment, and even the used high-end equipment is pretty expensive," Joshua thought to himself.

What does a creative-thinking, entrepreneurial free agent like him do?

Buy the broken ones.

He started small with some of the lesser expensive cameras and ones that he could afford to buy the broken ones of. He would repair them, sell them on eBay for a much higher price than he had paid, and would use that money to buy a broken version of the next level up.

At this time, he was already in school to continue his education on audio. Once he figured out that video was now where he saw his opportunity, he quickly changed his major to digital cinematography. All the while, he was still trying to work, and now, he had to get his feet wet with film. He did just that.

Joshua used his audio experience to get a gig as a boom operator for a feature film. One of the actors on set loved the energy and hustle he had and asked Joshua to be a part of a movie he wanted to do.

"I'll do it, but I have to be the director of photography."

And the actor agreed to it. Joshua now had his chance; all he needed was the right camera. He knew he wanted a RED cinema camera, yet he still didn't have the money to buy it.

He used his negotiation skills to talk down a seller for a broken one. As he started working to fix the camera, he realized that it was beyond repair, and he had no idea what he was doing. Luckily for him, his searches led to another differently broken camera. He was able to use the parts from the original broken one to fix the second, and suddenly he had a usable, high-quality cinema camera.

While fixing the cameras, he decided to record what he was doing and post it to YouTube. He became entrenched in the RED camera community and was known as the only one to figure out how to fix it. It even went as far as the president of RED sending him a note.

Joshua has created himself a business by fixing these cameras, and it's given him another source of revenue while he continues his filming career.

We can look at how Joshua was able to create the life and career he wanted because he thought outside the box. Instead of giving up on his mission, he took a problem, looked at it differently than others had before him, and built himself a career as a free agent.

HOW TO INNOVATE

Corporate philosopher, fellow at Boston Consulting Group, and founder of *Cartoonbase* Luc de Brabandere gives us some insight into creative thinking. "Thinking creatively means finding the divergent information and cross it from what we know to what we haven't thought about yet."[101]

---

101 Luc de Brabandere, Luc de, *Reinventing Creative Thinking*. TED, June 2015.

In other words, we take what we do know and apply those principles to something we haven't been able to do yet. Luc de Brabandere then breaks it down between two thoughts.

Deduction: starting from a limited set of existing hypotheses.

Induction: considering at least one new hypothesis.

Both of these lead to innovation, which he defines as continuous deduction out of the same box.[102]

One of *Fast Company's* one hundred most creative people in business and a top-rated professor at Wharton for five straight years, Adam Grant spent a decade studying originality only to find it much less complicated than he expected.[103] In his book, *Originals,* he describes the hallmark of originality as "rejecting the default and exploring whether a better option exists."[104]

That's what Joshua did. He could have readily accepted that he was not going to be a videographer and that film was not his future. Many others would.

---

102 Ibid.

103 Adam Grant, *Originals: How Non-Conformists Move the World*, New York, NY, Penguin Books, 2017. 7.

104 Ibid.

In what ways can you look at your line of work differently? Is there a way to improve your process, find a different set of clients that need your product?

We can apply the creative thinking lessons and connect them directly with how the world will see you. You can innovate as much as you can in one box, but eventually, space in that box will run out. That's the reality of business and is applied directly to free agents.

Just like large scale companies that have to continue to not only innovate but to adapt and bring their practices to different areas, free agents are at risk of being left in the dust. If you want to be on your own for twenty, thirty, or forty years, you must accept that you will continuously have to be on your toes and find new ways to differentiate yourself.

Both Luc de Brabandere and Grant seemingly agree that to separate yourself from the crowd, you must be a creative thinker or be at risk of blending in with everyone else. As a free agent, you can't risk blending in with the crowd because there will always be a cap on demand. Maybe you can continue to get by, but you don't want to just get by; you want to excel.

Luc de Brabandere provides this guidance to looking at yourself differently: [105]

---

105 "Luc de Brabandere, Reinventing Creative Thinking," June 2015, video, 14:00.

my products,

my services,

my activities

ARE AN EXAMPLE

Of...

Then finish that sentence in a way you haven't before.

Of course, this is all easier said than done. It takes time to really think about what your business is, not just on what you do. Applying creative thinking and innovation as a free agent can happen at all stages. Is it like Joshua at the beginning of his journey? Is it like Seinfeld and used directly in his craft? Or maybe you can apply it to the type of businesses you work for or how your company operates.

As a free agent, some obstacles may feel like they are too big to conquer. You're just one person, after all. But maybe, if we looked at some of our problems in a different way, we'd be able to find a new solution.

CHAPTER 7

YOU ARE THE BRAND

———

*"You can't build a reputation on
what you are going to do."*

— HENRY FORD

It's a Friday afternoon in spring of 2016. I'm leaving the cubicle I called home for eight hours every day, ready for the ensuing happy hour with coworkers who, like myself, were just a year out of college.

Our manager would wait towards the end of the cubicles with a fist bump ready for each of us. As we packed up and left for the weekend, he'd always tell us one thing.

"Protect your brand. Protect your brand."

It's easy to see why he told a bunch of early twenty-year-old's to not do something stupid over the weekend. It was the first time I realized how merely a reputation could mean so much for your career. One slip up, and it'd be stuck with you for your entire time at that firm, maybe longer.

In today's world, access to information, reviews, and communication with those you used to work with has never been easier, nor less discrete. Your brand follows you whether you like it or not.

What really goes into a personal brand? How can you influence or change it?

Specializing in one specific segment and becoming an expert may give you an initial boost in reputation and a leg up on those who might be considered more of a generalist. However, there is risk in specializing too deeply. Since technology is changing so rapidly, staying up to date and adjusting your brand will be critical.

Your brand is only as good as the demand for it.

If you don't become a specialist, you can take a generalist approach to work. Generalists are flexible. They can be pulled from one side of a business and moved directly to another with minimal problems. They are transferable.[106] All positive traits, but as a freelancer or contractor, can you afford to be a generalist?

That answer, of course, is, "it depends" but for free agents, knowing what you are and, most importantly, what you aren't

---

106 Martin Luenendonk, "The Ultimate Career Choice: Generalist vs. Specialist," Cleverism, March 23, 2016.

will be critical to growing the demand for your services. After all, people are coming to you to fill a specific need.

Entrepreneur, best-selling author, speaker, and freelancer Seth Godin believes the first rule of branding is simple: "keep your promises."[107]

I couldn't agree more.

If you try to take on more than you can handle or don't consistently bring your best work forward, you are at serious risk of hurting your reputation. Part of keeping your promises is understanding what you are as a business and what you are to the company you are working for.

Seth brought up a couple of points that are important for just that.

"If you're a freelancer, freelance,"

"If you're an entrepreneur, don't hire yourself."[108]

We will talk about this more in depth in the next chapter, but it's important to note. When you tell a company that you are a freelancer, you give them the expectation that you are going to be completing the tasks at hand and get paid for the work that you do.

---

107 Seth Godin, "The Simple First Rule of Branding and Marketing Anything (Even Yourself)," Seth's Blog, December 17, 2011.

108 Ibid.

So, when you feel like you are picking up more projects than you can handle and are forced to either subcontract or not deliver your best work, decide what kind of free agent you want to be.

A solopreneur may subcontract the work out to another person, but if you give your stamp of approval on the work that's not up to par, it will damage your brand. If you just want to freelance and you find yourself in this type of situation, think as a traditional business would.

If supply is fixed, as it is for freelancers, and businesses can't keep up with demand, what does a good business do to get back to equilibrium? They raise prices.

Raising prices means you are in demand. You're a free agent; when you set out to work on your own, that's what you wanted. You want to have a steady stream of jobs, make enough money to live the life you want, and not have to answer to a boss.

Entrepreneurs are not freelancers. They get in trouble when they are the ones trying to do all the work or the business model relies on the ability of the founder to do much of the work. That's not building a business, that's freelancing at an unsustainable scale.

One change we see more of when it comes to younger workers is the desire never to have a corporate job and, instead, start on your own without any pedigree to build off of. How do you become an expert in something that you haven't had previous experience in?

Let me introduce you to Stefanie.

I first met Stefanie at my previous job. Stefanie was thirty years old and doing a cross-country speaking tour for the Fortune 500 company I was working for, talking specifically about millennials and money.

Without a background in finance, she's been featured in Forbes, Fox Business, The Wall Street Journal, and countless other news sources, all discussing this topic of millennials and their money. When it came to the discussion around branding, I thought who better to discuss it with than Stefanie.

Stefanie grew up always wanting to be an actor. When it came time to go to college, she chose a school in New York to be right in the center of everything and follow her passion for the stage. After the years of hard work, she graduated and fulfilled her dream of being a professional actor.

Along with being a professional theatre actor, she was also a waitress, babysitter, personal assistant, and any other "survival job" that she could find. She was living the dream.

Except she wasn't.

Stefanie took an in-depth look in the mirror and thought there had to be a more viable way to have a sustainable career, while still not having to let go of her dream of being a on the stage.

So, she began writing. She started a blog and spent her days reaching out to others she found on the internet to connect about writing content and seeing if anyone needed any free-lance writers. Initially, some of her first blog posts paid her a mere $20, pennies compared to what she'd get for a post today.

"For me, the shift into freelancing was actually better than the world I was coming from since it was so inherently unstable, to begin with."

Stability is something she craved in her finances, but she knew nothing about money. So, she took some classes on it.

After learning about how wrong the things she wanted to spend her money on were, it made it difficult to relate to the information she received. Finance was a personal pain point of hers and she thought it might be for others as well. So, she began writing about it.

She wrote honestly about the unstable income she had as an actor with multiple survival jobs. Her acting background taught her how to genuinely connect with people, and combined with the content she was producing, people could relate to her.

What initially was $20 blog posts started to be $50, then $100, and so on, and suddenly she wasn't having to work those survival jobs as often. As soon as she could, she completely welcomed this freelancing lifestyle to replace the income from the survival jobs.

Looking around at her friends that had what she deemed as "exciting careers," she saw that they had unique skill sets that don't always seem related, but they not only made it work, they made it their trademark. In the case of Stefanie, her ability to blend her acting skills with this world of personal finance led her to the speaking opportunities at multiple Fortune 500 firms.

"I think it's a new way of creating value, especially as we're moving into a world in which so much could be automated … it's going to be more and more important to take some of the left brain and right brain and find that intersection because that's the stuff that only people can do."

Her quote is a direct insight into how she branded herself to come up with her offering. At the time, millennials were just starting to have a more significant influence on the world, yet there wasn't anyone who could talk about personal finance with them. So, she wrote a book titled, *The Broke and Beautiful Life: Small Town Budget, Big City Dreams.*

It was now 2015, and the book launched her into a world she hadn't been in before. By being one of the first authors of the millennial money genre, she was immediately garnering requests to appear on TV. Living in New York City coupled with her willingness and availability gave her initial success on TV. Studios would call her and ask to do interviews during off times, such as on and around Christmas, and since she was right down the street, she'd gladly accept and be on TV in no time.

The appearances on TV and being an author of one of the first books on millennial money ultimately led to those speaking engagements and partnerships with Fortune 500 firms.

"So much of this is about the right time, the right moment, being in the right place, and then showing up every damn day until you get it right. It's not sexy."

Stefanie is now setting her sights on other topics that are related to but not explicitly focused on millennial money. She hopes to take her ability to see the bigger world around her and use it to find a niche area she can focus on and, once again, become a thought leader in a new field.

While not everyone reading this book may want to become a thought leader or be on a stage, Stefanie teaches us that finding a subject that you can be an expert or leader on is critical to making it on your own. Businesses hire freelancers and contractors to fill a void that they can't fill internally, so finding that void and filling it yourself will ultimately lead to success as a free agent.

The niche that Stefanie made for herself was directly related to her successes. She not only writes about personal finance; she writes about millennials and women and their finances. Being specific has its benefits, but what if you create a niche that is no longer important or at the forefront of business?

A personal brand or reputation can undoubtedly change, but it also can be broader than a specific skill. Your story could be your brand, and what you are looking to accomplish helps tell that story. Stefanie wanted to bring personal finance to millennials and talk about it in a way that helps them understand, not punish them for valuing different things than their parents.

WIDTH OF A BRAND

Stefanie's story shows a narrower approach to creating your brand than some others we have seen. Similar to Morgan, the wedding photographer from the passion chapter, Stefanie found a small field that she could succeed in with her set of skills.

That's just one approach. The other method would be to find a skill that is transferable between fields or industries and make it your own. That's the way we saw Vanessa and Holly enact in their careers. They each had their own skill. Vanessa is an event planner, and Holly is a communications director; both take their skills to a variety of clients and industries.

Let's dive deeper into this.

"I don't know if I could ever go back," April shared with me her thoughts of returning to corporate America during our conversation. "It's just so satisfying."

Some people are born to be in a particular profession. Some are seemingly destined to become doctors or lawyers; others may be artists or actors. April was destined for a career in sales.

As a child desperate for Christmas money, April would knock mistletoes out of trees, go back home, hot glue them together, and then go door to door selling them.

Early on, it was clear that April was skilled in sales, even though she may not have always realized it.

She spent her high school and college days in Germany and found it challenging to use her degree, so when she came back to the States, she tried her hand at nursing school. After finishing, she found herself pregnant with her second child and right in the middle of a lengthy divorce process.

It was time for some serious self-reflection.

"What am I best at?"

She was best at sales, and she knew it.

She took her background as a nurse and transitioned into pharmaceutical sales. While pharma sales were undoubtedly not her passion, she loved the process and found a way to get behind what she was selling.

"I figured that if you're good at sales, and you can be passionate about whatever it is that you're selling, then you can sell anything."

April found ways to become passionate about what she was selling and was able to then take those skills to other fields, such as financial services. While she enjoyed the perks and all of the pats on the back she received for being a successful saleswoman in corporate America, she was looking to find a different satisfaction.

That's when April and her new life and business partner started their own company. With no desire to risk everything, she helped out the business while continuing her sales role at the Fortune 500 corporations she was working for.

As she operated her side hustle for a few years, she became more ingrained in the startup community. Then, April had the opportunity to become an interim Chief Revenue Officer for a startup.

"I'm going to go help this startup compete against HR industry giants in a way they would never be able to."

And that she did.

She was directly behind a startup now meeting with Fortune 100 companies because of the sales strategies she helped implement. After that initial consulting success, she found other friends who were launching companies came calling as well. She decided to make the switch and leave the benefit-laden corporate job to work for herself full-time.

April now consults for several organizations, including one that promotes minority women entrepreneurs by putting on pitch competitions with venture capital dollars going to the winners.

She loved this company and was extremely passionate about the topic. She reached out to the founder on LinkedIn and expressed her desire to help. The founder's initial impression was that April knew a bunch of rich people and had a background in non-profit fundraising.

That, of course, was not true.

A few weeks after being brought on, April was collaborating with the founder when she learned of these initial impressions.

April's excitement for this project had led her to, without thinking about it, not send over her contract, scope of the business, and all related items to the organization. The miscommunication of her role made her future with the organization unsure.

While this story ended up working out for April in the end, and she was able to pivot and showcase how she could help the organization, it almost didn't, and we can learn from it.

A brand covers more than just the image you convey but also how you operate your business. For April, she had a set way to begin her work with clients that set appropriate expectations and outlined the scope of what she can do in helping companies.

Your scope ends up defining who you are as a business and the value you provide for a company. April is a sales consultant and brings with her years of success at all sizes of businesses. She then carries her defined scope to every organization she works with.

For those looking to find your brand and the scope of your work, April's advice to fellow free agents was simple: "Find who that perfect, target client would be and ask them if they have a need for this and what it would do for them."

Becoming a free agent allows you to tailor yourself to the space you want to work in and ultimately control the work you want to do. Sales allowed April to take a skill she is outstanding at and apply it to causes she loves, creating the lifestyle she had always wanted.

Stefanie and April found different ways to apply branding to themselves and took significantly different paths to get there. In Stefanie's case, she narrowed her focus and put enough content out there to get a book deal and continued talking about one prevalent issue. April had a vast array of experiences within sales but used her skills to cross many different sectors and sizes of business.

Your brand and reputation are what will carry you through independent work. When deciding what you want your image to be, consider how narrow the niche you are creating can be. While being an expert can yield results immediately, consider the long-term prospects and the goals you have for yourself.

PART 3

FIND YOUR PATH

CHAPTER 8

UNDERSTANDING YOURSELF

—

*"In any moment of decision, the best thing
you can do is the right thing, the next
best thing is the wrong thing, and the
worst thing you can do is nothing."*

— THEODORE ROOSEVELT

It's 1999 in Los Angeles, California. As the world was preparing for Y2k and the impending computer scare, Dante was a teenager working for his mom. She recently started a company that ran the facilities for focus groups in the area. When she needed help, Dante and his brother would "pinch hit" as an interviewer or moderator, and he spent a lot of days working on market research. It's where he first saw what it was like to be a part of a small business.

After helping out his mom for a few years, he and his brother took that experience and started their own business doing qualitative research.

Along the way, he found himself being drawn in by politics and considered dabbling in it. After graduating from college, he continued his market research while also working as a grassroots organizer and at any other political gig he could clamor his way onto.

Then the great recession hit in 2008.

Left without much money saved and the family business struggling, Dante didn't have many options. He found himself awake at night, panicking over what to do and how to survive this devastating economy. Then it hit him.

"You know, rich kids in LA's west side still need their help with their Latin classes in their private high schools."

Dante reached back into his background and started a company doing Latin and other academic tutoring. Making $80 an hour, he saw it as a way to keep a roof over his head until the private sector businesses rebounded.

And even as business rebounded, he still was working to find his way deeper into politics. Then on Halloween night of 2014, he packed up his bags and made the cross-country trip to Washington, D.C. to be with his girlfriend who had already been working and living there. Initially without a job, he spent the next few months searching and was able to get hired as a congressional communications director on Capitol Hill.

When he started on the hill, he realized this was the first time he ever had a full-time job that wasn't for a family member. It was a unique experience that he wanted to make the most of. So, he found himself continuously working, with late nights and little time for a social life. The consistency of waking up at the same time, arriving at the office at the same time, and not knowing when he'd be going home was a lot to get used to.

Then, after the house majority flipped in 2018, his congressional office decided it needed to let go of some of its senior communications staff to make way for new legislative staff now that they were in control.

"Freelancer life and politics life resemble each other in many ways; there is always an end date," Dante told me.

He had worked on the hill for three and a half years and wrapped up his time knowing that the eleven or twelve hour daily grind lifestyle wasn't for him. He no longer wanted to sacrifice his personal life because of work.

"I think I actually want to continue doing this entrepreneurial thing and be able to work from my pajamas and not have to, you know, cater to jerks,"

Dante found that he was ready to return to the independent workforce, and he knew just how to do it.

Freelancers like Dante have been able to move in and out of freelancing without much difficulty by accepting new opportunities when they come. He had been self-employed before, and it allowed him to take on different roles when he wanted to, like working for a congressman. It also gave him a skill set that he could bring back to his freelancing business.

If you decide to make that jump into self-employment and things don't work out, or even if they work out better than you expected, you can always go back and find a traditional job. Whether you find a great opportunity, need the benefits, or struggle on your own, as much as work is changing, it hasn't completely changed yet.

Because traditional employment is there for you, if you're thinking about becoming a free agent, ask yourself one question.

Why?

"WHY" MATTERS

It's Monday morning, and your alarm won't seem to stop ringing, no matter how often you hit snooze. We've all been there before and have had that "I don't want to go to work today" feeling.

Traditional employees usually have to begrudgingly get out of bed and start moving on with their day. What if there was a way for you to start the morning at your pace instead of having to be in the office at eight o'clock in the morning on the dot?

That brings us to the motivation of being a free agent. Have you lost your job and are turning to self-employment as an option, or are you making this decision strategically? If we look at this as a strategic decision, many factors could be at play.

Are you like the seventy-four percent of full-time freelancers who say a significant reason to freelance is the ability to work from the location of your choosing?[109]

Do you think you can make more money than you currently do, like twenty-nine percent of full-time freelancers?[110]

Maybe, you are closer to the end of your career, and you desire to work less as a way to retire without completely retiring. More and more boomers are looking to do just that, and often becoming an independent consultant is a way to make that possible.[111]

No matter the reason, to be successful on your own, you need to understand what drove this decision and what you are looking to get out of it.

Well, known freelance designer and writer, Paul Jarvis authored the book *Company of One* after finding that people who start businesses to work for themselves seem to find an

---

109 "Freelancing in America: 2019," *Upwork/Freelancers Union*, LinkedIn SlideShare (September 23, 2019).

110 Ibid.

111 Harriet Edleson, "Boomers Want to Work, Transition to Retirement," *AARP*, April 3, 2019.

external pressure to grow their business, even when that's not the original goal.[112]

After sending out one of his weekly newsletters containing the subject: Why he didn't care about growth, the replies came pouring in.[113]

"I thought I was the only one who felt this way."

In one form or another, his subscribers admitted that they felt comfortable with their business not growing but faced pressure from outside forces to try to grow it.[114]

In reality, there aren't many podcasts or books available for self-employed workers that say, "be comfortable on your own and live the life you set out on your own to live." Paul noticed this, so naturally, he wrote a book about it.

After his book was published, he appeared on "the Minimalists podcast," explaining, "we start a business with these intentions of wanting more freedom, and we just keep adding more and more responsibilities because we think we want to legitimize it."[115]

---

112   Paul Jarvis. *Company of One: Why Staying Small Is the next Big Thing for Business.* Boston, MA, Mariner Books, Houghton Mifflin Harcourt, 2020.

113   Elaine Pofeldt, "Want to Keep Your Business Small? Paul Jarvis Is Your Man," Forbes. Forbes Magazine, January 17, 2019.

114   Ibid.

115   The Minimalists Podcast, and Paul Jarvis, "www.theminimalists.com,"

Paul brings up a great point and his explanation of why more and more people are moving towards this free agent lifestyle. Freedom.[116]

Twenty-seven percent of full-time freelancers were driven to freelancing by realizing that the free lifestyle was the one they wanted.[117] They want freedom from one employer. They want to be able to pick their kids up from school at three o'clock in the afternoon and start working again on their couch at eight o'clock at night.

Autonomy in your work is a powerful thing, and now more than ever people are looking for their opportunity to be free from the constraints of traditional employment.

GET COMFORTABLE WITH THE UNCOMFORTABLE

Imagine waking up one morning fully rested, and you look at your alarm. "Oh no, it's nine o'clock in the morning!"

Then, you realize there is no need to freak out and run to get your work clothes on. You crawl out of bed, slowly turn on the coffee machine and pull up to your computer. You are in no rush because you don't have to go anywhere; walking the dog is all you have on your calendar that day.

Sounds like a vacation.

---

116 Ibid.

117 "Freelancing in America: 2019," *Upwork/Freelancers Union*, LinkedIn SlideShare, September 23, 2019.

It's now been a couple of weeks since your last contract, and you're still impatiently waiting for the check to get mailed to you. You've got a mortgage and car payment due next week, and you're starting to wonder if you made the biggest mistake of your life when you read *The Free Agent Mindset* by Scott Jones and decided to go out on your own.

That brings us to potentially the most significant decision factor for looking seriously at becoming a free agent.

Money. Not just having an emergency fund, but confidently talking about money with your clients.

For many people, and possibly you, the money conversation is a dreaded conversation to have.

Americans HATE talking about money. So much so that thirty-four percent of couples can't even agree on how much salary their other half makes.[118] People are more comfortable talking about marriage problems, mental illness, drug addiction, race, sex, politics, and religion than they are about money.[119]

If you can't even talk about salaries with your partner, how are you supposed to communicate your price tag to a company that wants to hire you? Not only that, but if and when they push back, you need to have the confidence in yourself to not let them talk you down on price.

---

118 "The 2018 Fidelity Investments Couples & Money Study," Fidelity Investments, 2018.

119 "Confronting the Money Taboo," Capital Group, December 2018.

What does this look like in practice, and how can you better prepare yourself down the line?

Let's talk to Kim.

Kim is now a freelance communications consultant after deciding to go out on her own a few years ago.

She did so without really having a complete idea of what her client situation was going to look like or how she was going to get more clients.

But eventually, she got her first one. And then another one.

Then, she found what turned out to be one of her main clients, and the company had a cause she felt very passionate about and was really excited to work for.

Her client was a workplace consultant that was extremely focused around pay equity, gender equality, and everything else to make workplaces better. When Kim initially proposed her initial pay rate, it was too much for her client. She had to negotiate.

In her field, she found that she often had to convince people that they should be doing communications and didn't want to put one of her favorite clients at risk by a complicated negotiation.

After settling on a pay rate, she was hesitant to bring it up again, even though she felt like the project needed more hours on it.

Flash forward about a year, she was facing pressure from her client on the work that she was producing. Kim knew she had to have an uncomfortable conversation. She went to her client and said, "we're not accomplishing what you want because of the fact that you're not paying enough."

For many of us, this type of situation is a horror story and is reason enough to stay in your corporate job and get your annual two percent raise. In Kim's case, she received the hours she needed and has a stronger relationship than she previously had with that particular client.

Asking for a raise or a reevaluation of your worth is not easy.

That's not just for free agents either; only thirty-seven percent of employees have asked for a raise from their current employer.[120]

Probably not because the employer rewards them every chance that they get.

We know that talking about money is taboo, and asking for it is even more awkward; so, how do free agents get to a rate that both parties are comfortable with?

"It's really important to make sure that the clients and the people you surround yourself with are like-minded in terms of paying people what they're worth," Kim told me.

---

120 "How to Ask for A Raise," PayScale, Accessed May 9, 2020.

Both she and I have heard horror stories from free agents about never getting paid for a contract or clients trying to change the agreement after the fact. It's not an easy world out there.

Bottom line: Find good clients, not just clients.

AM I MAKING THE RIGHT DECISION?

Going out on your own is one of the biggest bets you can make in your life. It's a bet on yourself, and you hold all the cards. For many of us, betting sounds a lot like gambling, and gambling sounds risky.

A bet means "to stake on the outcome of an issue or the performance of a contestant."[121]

Only this time, you are the contestant. When you are becoming a free agent, you are putting down a wager tied to the ultimate success of your new work arrangement.

So, what should go into the decision?

First and foremost, be objective. You have to take the emotion out of a decision like this to properly evaluate your personal situation. Are you financially ready? Are your skills needed? Most importantly, are you mentally prepared?

Don't take it from me though, let's learn our betting techniques from the only woman to have won the World Series of

---

121 *Merriam-Webster.com Dictionary*, s.v. "bet," accessed June 3, 2020.

Poker Tournament of Champions. She has also been awarded a National Science Foundation Fellowship to study cognitive psychology at the University of Pennsylvania. Her name is Annie Duke.

In Annie's latest book, *Thinking in Bets: Making Smarter Decisions When You Don't Have All the Facts*, she discusses the tendency for people to equate bad results as making a wrong decision.[122]

When there are factors out of your control, you can only make the best decision with the hand you are dealt and hope for a good result. Annie starts off the book with an example that almost 115 million people can relate to: the 2015 Super Bowl XLIX game between the New England Patriots and Seattle Seahawks.[123]

In what still is the highest viewed Super Bowl of all time, it is most known for Seattle's head coach Pete Carrol's controversial decision to throw the ball while they were on the Patriot's one-yard line.[124] With the game on the line, instead of handing the ball off to Marshawn "Beast Mode" Lynch, the play call was for quarterback Russell Wilson to throw a pass.

The pass was subsequently intercepted by Patriot's cornerback Malcolm Butler and just like that, the Patriots won their

---

122 Annie Duke, *Thinking in Bets: Making Smarter Decisions When You Don't Have All the Facts*, NY, NY. Portfolio/Penguin, 2019, 5-8.

123 Christina Gough, "Number of Super Bowl Viewers (TV) 2019," *Statista*, February 10, 2020.

124 Ibid.

fourth Super Bowl of the century, and that play went on to be one of the most criticized play calls in NFL history.

"Worst play-call in Super Bowl history will forever alter perception of Seahawks, Patriots" The Washington Post exclaimed.[125]

Or was it?

Annie's argument is that yes, the outcome was horrible for the Seahawks, but that doesn't automatically mean it was the wrong decision. She references analysis from Benjamin Morris of FiveThirtyEight.com and Brian Burke of Slate.com that Pete Carrol made a decision that had resulted in an interception only about two percent of the time.[126]

The much more likely scenario would be a result of a touchdown or, at worst, an incomplete pass, which would have resulted in another couple of opportunities to run the ball if Pete Carrol felt better about it.

In poker, the best players in the world bet according to what the odds are telling them. The best initial hand a player can get is pocket aces. That initial hand will win the round seventy percent of the time.[127]

---

125 Mark Maske, "'Worst Play-Call in Super Bowl History' Will Forever Alter Perception of Seahawks, Patriots," *The Washington Post*, February 2, 2015.

126 Annie Duke, *Thinking in Bets: Making Smarter Decisions When You Don't Have All the Facts.* NY, NY, Portfolio/Penguin, 2019, 5-8.

127 "With a 52-Card Deck, What Are the Odds of Drawing a Pair of Jacks?" Wizard of Odds, Wizard of Odds, Accessed May 11, 2020.

It sounds like it's time to go all in.

The problem is, even if the player is in the best possible situation and does everything correctly, they will still lose thirty percent of the time.[128] They can't afford to look back and think they did something wrong. They know that luck is not always on their side.

We can take this advice through many aspects of our life. Judging your decisions and not their outcomes is a difficult change to the mindsets of humans, but a change successful people must make.

How does it affect free agents?

When you're thinking about going out on your own, you know it's not easy to succeed. Only fifty-six percent of new businesses make it to the fifth year.[129] That doesn't give you a ton of confidence. However, when we dig deeper, we find out that forty-two percent found that there wasn't a market for their services, so it wasn't a great idea from the beginning.[130]

One way that many free agents increase their odds of success is by finding a free agent mentor. Having someone in your corner to help educate you on the business elements that you are new to only enables you to get comfortable in your unique work situation. As much as self-employment relies

128 Ibid.

129 Matt Mansfield, "STARTUP STATISTICS – The Numbers You Need to Know," Small Business Trends, March 28, 2019.

130 Ibid.

on being self-sufficient, having someone who has been there and done that is incredibly valuable.

The concept is common to that of a mentor that you'd see in the corporate setting, where fifty-six percent of people say they have had a professional mentor.[131] On average, the mentor and mentee speak four hours a month and have been working together for 3.3 years.[132] So, it's not about constant communication but a focused conversation on how to operate yourself as a business.

Look for free agent mentors who can help you figure out your pricing, best practices, and where to begin with taxes. With technology today, it's become more accessible for people to find other people to connect with, so be sure to take advantage of that.

The difficulty for free agents and mentors comes because, at some level, you are in direct competition with many of those who you'd want to mentor you. To solve this, you may have to look outside your field to find those who you aren't competing with or find someone who is attracting different types of clients.

That mentor can also help you in your decision-making process. Before you go out on your own, learn a little more about what it's really like and develop a process that you feel comfortable with.

---

131 "Study Explores Professional Mentor-Mentee Relationships in 2019," Olivet Nazarene University, 2019.

132 Ibid.

"Resulting" will pop its head much more than just the initial move into being a free agent. Did you do everything right to try and win a big contract only to fall short? It's going to happen at some point, so stick with the process you develop. One of the more significant mistakes a new free agent can make is letting their confidence swing one way or another based on the results of a bid and completely overhauling how they operate after one miss.

Focus on the process of making the decision rather than what ultimately happens. If you can look back and say you made the best decision with the facts laid out before you, accept the outcome and move on.

CHAPTER 9

HEDGE YOUR BET

"Busy is a decision."

— DEBBIE MILLMAN, FOUNDER AND HOST
OF DESIGN MATTERS PODCAST[133]

"I want to start a brewery," Jeff said to his then-wife, Kim.[134]

It was 1991 Fort Collins, Colorado, in the basement of an electrical engineer and a social worker.

Jeff, the electrical engineer, had traveled on a mountain bike journey throughout Belgium a few years prior. He fell in love with the creativity, the fruits, and the experimentation of

---

133 Timothy Ferris. *Tribe of Mentors: Short Life Advice from the Best in the World*. Boston: Houghton Mifflin Harcourt Publishing Company, 2018. P. 24.

134 "Live Episode! New Belgium Brewing Company: Kim Jordan," *How I Built This with Guy Raz*, NPR, September 10, 2018.

Belgian beer, and he was adapting it to the beer he brewed at home.

The neighbors loved it, and so did everyone else.

But the 1990s were a much different time for craft beer. There were many times where Jeff and Kim would offer to bring beer to friend's party only to be told there's "no need to, we have a keg of Coors Light."

Disheartening as it was, they pressed on.

Although the craft brew revolution hadn't quite started yet, they saw signs of a changing beer landscape. In Fort Collins, brewpubs were beginning to pop up, and there was a brewery that made draft beer for bars and restaurants.

Kim and Jeff saw a significant opening within the industry: packaged beer.

The newlyweds decided to take a second mortgage out on their house, maxed out every credit card they could, and started a brewery in their basement.

They weren't looking at a business with any expectations that it would someday have a billion-dollar valuation, but rather one they could make a living off of.

While hiking in Rocky Mountain National Park during the very beginning stages of their brewery, Kim and Jeff discussed being business and life partners. They decided that if they were indeed going to open a brewery, these are the goals they wanted to achieve.

1. Produce world-class Belgian style beers
2. Be environmental stewards
3. Promote beer culture
4. Have fun

None of the goals were to scale and fit to become the third-largest craft brewer in the country, eventually distributing beers to all fifty states. Regardless, they went for it.

Jeff quit his job and became the "brewmaster" at their little basement brewery that they fittingly named, New Belgium. When told the name of their flagship amber ale, Fat Tire, people scoffed at it and begged them to find something better. Instead, they stuck with it.

Kim stayed on as a social worker keeping key benefits such as insurance; plus, they also still needed the cash flow. With one young child already and trying to have another, she would spend her off days managing order flow. The initial customers were both bars and restaurants, as well as independent liquor stores.

At the time, there was nothing else that was similar in the marketplace. Kim would call the customers in the morning, go drop off the beer in the afternoon, pick up her kid from school, and finish the deliveries in the early evenings.

"Poor kid knew the town by the liquor stores for a while."[135]

The beginnings of New Belgium can tell us a lot about the mindsets of people who decide to go all in on self-employment, while also hedging a bit. Self-employment for a lot of couples is a team activity.

Many self-employed workers have a spouse or partner that has a more regular job, especially in today's world where health insurance is such a high expense. Having both spouses as independent workers will present unique challenges and added costs that the family will have to be aware of.

Kim and Jeff saw the opportunity and took a chance. Their thought process falls right in line with everything we have talked about to this point. They looked at the opportunity in front of them, were creative with what their product was, hedged a little, and went for it. They weren't initially entrepreneurs or the business progressives that they (especially Kim) are known for now.

"There was no way I'm going to tell my brand-new husband that he has to keep working. You have to go to that benchtop and do that thing you do because we have to have this paycheck."[136]

They were just a husband and wife looking to create a new journey together and enjoy the life they had in front of them.

---

135 Ibid
136 Ibid

As much fun as it sounds, it may be too late to start your craft brewery and have success doing so. According to the Brewers Association, the overall beer market actually fell 0.8 percent in 2018, and the previously rapid increase of craft beer drinking seems to be slowing down.[137]

The good news is there are a lot more options to be self-employed than opening a brewery. Use the set of skills that you already have and find the void you can fill and boom, you have yourself a business.

If we use Kim and Jeff from New Belgium, we can see the two different approaches.

Kim hedged her bet by maintaining her full-time job as a social worker. She had great benefits her young family needed while they were starting the brewery. Giving up those benefits would have been extremely damaging to the family if the brewery didn't work out, not to mention expensive to replicate.

On the other hand, Jeff had two things going for him to be the one who goes "all in." First and foremost, he was the mastermind behind the beer. He created Fat Tire and knew how to make a delicious Belgian beer. Second, he was the one without excellent benefits. Quitting his job didn't have the same influence on the family that Kim or both of them leaving would have.

---

137 "National Beer Sales & Production Data," Brewers Association, Accessed May 12, 2020.

THE SIDE HUSTLE

Does the thought of going to your office one day, telling your boss those magic words, "I quit!" excite you, or does it terrify you?

If you have a business in mind that you want to start, you have a couple of different approaches to consider. Do you keep doing what you're doing and add another layer of work to your day, or do you go all in?

While not the subject of many motivational quotes on Pinterest, starting your venture on the side decreases your risk, allows you to test the waters, and ultimately give self-employment a test-run.

It's also a way to gain different experiences, try new things, and hopefully earn some extra cash.

As it turns out, twenty-five percent of Americans have a side business.[138] While it would be fair to expect these side hustles to be mostly gig-working millennials, surprisingly, only twenty-six percent of side hustlers are millennials.[139]

People aren't just doing these jobs for an extra paycheck, either. Forty percent of those millennial side hustlers see their business as something that they will likely turn into their full-time job someday — potentially adding many

---

138 "The Hartford's 2018 Side Business Survey," The Hartford, September 2018.

139 Ibid.

more to the already fifty-seven million freelancers already in business.[140]

The side hustle is not without its faults. Many people use gigs to try to earn an extra paycheck, and that typically relies upon becoming a contractor for a company like Uber or Postmates.

And while driving for Uber certainly has its merits and fits under the side hustle umbrella, I'd like to focus on those who are thinking about freelancing full-time or starting their own business but have chosen to only do so part-time.

In the last chapter, we talked about betting on yourself; this would be hedging that bet.

While it's most often associated with investing, hedging your career certainly has its benefits. It's a way to limit the downside risk if things don't go the way you planned. Hedging sacrifices some of the upside to limit the downside.

For a free agent, you aren't committing to a new lifestyle, and you're still able to maintain some of the more useful aspects of full-time work. You get your healthcare, a consistent paycheck, and know what your job looks like every day. You are just dipping your toes into the free agent pool, not yet jumping in.

---

140 "Freelancing in America: 2019," *Upwork/Freelancers Union*, LinkedIn SlideShare, September 23, 2019.

Working a side hustle that you are thinking about taking full-time may add stress as it involves working more hours. There are trade-offs that you individually will have to look at and decide what's important to you.

If you think outside the box, the side hustle can be quite powerful for your career as well. In the book, *The Side Hustle: How to Turn Your Spare Time into $1000 a Month or More*, Nick Loper, the founder of Side Hustle Nation, mentions a few things that a side hustle allows you to do:[141]

1. Build Skills
2. Build Security
3. Build Income
4. Build Freedom

After all, we aren't adding this extra work for no reason. The key to a side hustle is understanding what you are using it for. Using a side hustle to build freedom puts you well on your way to be a full-time free agent; you are just doing it in a more mentally relaxed fashion. It allows you to test the waters, make sure you have a market for your services, build a reputation in the area, and see what it's like to be on your own while not having to risk your current livelihood.

KEEPING ALL DOORS OPEN

Morgan has envisioned herself going to medical school and becoming a doctor for as long as she could remember. She

---

141 Nick Loper, *The Side Hustle: How to Turn Your Spare Time into $1000 a Month or More*, Independently published.

went to an excellent college to study biology on the pre-med path, well on her way to becoming a general pediatrician. One morning, in the summer before her senior year, she woke up thinking, "I don't want to do this anymore."

After mulling on it for a few days, she brought her change of heart up to her dad at the dinner table.

After paying for the first three years of college, her dad was initially curious with the sudden change.

"Med school was always your plan," he said. "What do you want to do now?"

"I know I don't want to go to med school, but I don't know what to do, what I want to do,"

It's important to know that Morgan grew up loving to write. She was the editor-in-chief of her high school newspaper. When she went to college, even with everything encompassed by biology and pre-med, she still made time to become editor-in-chief at the university's pre-med newspaper.

Even more, she was an editor at LAYoga magazine in the summer in between her junior and senior year.

"What are you going to do?" her father continued during that fateful dinner the summer before her senior year."

"I don't know, Dad"

"What do you like to do?" He kept on.

"Well, I really love content, and I really love healthcare," she answered back.

"So, do that!"

Until that point, Morgan hadn't realized that putting content and healthcare together was an option for her.

After graduating with her original biology and pre-med degree, she interned at a healthcare startup. She then took her first full-time job working as an entry-level writer, not making a lot of money but getting by.

She was approached by a friend of hers from college who was working for a Customer Relationship Management (CRM) startup and asked her if she'd like to join as a freelance writer with them.

"I was like, 'yeah, sure!'"

At the time he asked her, she actually didn't know what a CRM was. Feeling lucky to get her first job, she went with the attitude, "I'm sure I can figure it out, right?"

Morgan's descent into freelancing isn't unlike most others. The first client is so essential and seemingly always the most memorable. She's now been freelancing on the side for five years and has continued her focus on healthcare.

Her full-time job is in content strategy, and now she's also seen her freelancing roles lean a little bit more towards strategy, yet still hasn't taken the plunge into full-fledged freelancing, just yet.

That brings us back to hedging.

Two of the more difficult things to have as a freelancer is a company and the support system in place to begin freelancing while staying at a full-time job. Companies aren't always going to like that.

After all, "if you have more time to work, why aren't you working more for us" is an attitude that all too many employers have.

In unfortunate scenarios, they are going to see the situation as someone who has more time to give to their current job and is not going to be comfortable allowing you to have a side hustle. Many companies also will be worried that you are going to start stealing from some of their client pool, intellectual property, office supplies, which are much more valid concerns.

To prevent some of the potential issues that come from freelancing as a side gig, here are a few tips.

1. Be upfront. One piece of advice that Morgan took to heart when she continued freelancing on the side was being transparent with her boss and her company. While she performed similar work during the day as when she freelanced, they were never to the same type of clients. Even though she has had some bosses question it, as long as you are doing the same quality of work (easier said than done)

and your contract doesn't state otherwise, you should be good to go.

2. Never use anything from the company to help your business. Everyone has done this, right? Printed a personal item off at work or taken a pen or two? Sure, but you now operate as a company, and you don't want to give the company you currently are working for any reason to have problems with you.

3. Manage your time to the best of your abilities. Remember, this is your side gig, and there are only so many jobs that you can take on when you still have another full-time job to perform at. Don't take on what you can't do, and remember you still have a life outside of work that you need to be cognizant of.

Morgan is using freelancing as a way to allow herself to gain different experiences, earn some extra cash, and to continue to do something she enjoys, write.

Which is perfectly okay!

We talked about branding ourselves as free agents. Well, if you are not ready to brand yourself as XYZ, then maybe it's time to take a step back and ask yourself if going all in on freelancing is right for you.

As long as there is a market for your expertise, you're in a great position. If that runs out, you would have to pivot into something else. That is much more challenging to do when you are attached to one field.

The companies you contract for, your website, and even the government are all going to need to know what your business is, and if you are younger like Morgan, or just not ready to go all-in, take a step back, earn some extra cash, and enjoy your life.

Hedging is a safe and comfortable way to approach being a free agent. But what if that's not your style? If you're desperate to get started, well, let's talk about what it means to jump in.

CHAPTER 10

JUMPING IN

"If you're offered a seat on a rocket ship,
don't ask what seat! Just get on."

— SHERYL SANDBERG, COO OF FACEBOOK

In his memoir, Phil Knight describes his coming of age as nothing special.[142] He grew up in a typical family for the time, and his father exemplified it all. He describes his father as craving respectability above all else. It was post-war America, and a person's reputation meant everything.

Phil grew up just outside of Portland, Oregon. He attended the University of Oregon and was a three-time letterman in track. He loved to run and loved to compete. After graduating from Oregon, he had a brief stint in the Army while the Korean war came to an end.

---

142 Phil Knight. *Shoe Dog.* New York, NY, Scribner, 2016.

Afterward, in keeping with being on the safe and respectable path he was on, Phil attended Stanford Graduate School of Business.

For a project in his entrepreneurship class, Phil argued that if Japanese camera companies, such as Canon or Nikon, could disrupt the camera market from the typical German manufacturers, the same could happen with running shoes. At the time, Adidas and Puma dominated the running shoe market.

His classmates looked on to his presentation with their sleepy and bored eyes. However, his professor liked it, and he received an A.

But that wasn't enough. Phil admitted that he had never worked as intensely on a project as he had this one, and that fire continued to burn long after he completed the class.

Now a Stanford M.B.A. graduate, he was back at his parents' house trying to figure out what he wanted to do with his life. Lingering in his head was the excellent shoe idea. "How could he make it work?" he thought.

He also thought about the alternative. He had begun working for an accounting firm and despised it. He craved more; he wanted the competition and excitement of a race and knew the shoe idea would give him that.

He decided to give it a try.

He had never been outside the United States, and he questioned how he could be an importer of Japanese shoes if he'd never seen the country.

So, he decided to fly across the world. His father gave him some money to "complete his education" and off he went. There was no business plan nor an outline of his company. Nothing.

When he arrived in Japan after a couple of detours along the way, he maneuvered his way into a meeting with Onitsuka, makers of the Tiger shoe and now known as Asics.

"I'd like to be the sole importer of your shoes in the Western United States," Phil told the executive.

"What company do you work for again?" The man replied.

Phil realized he hadn't thought this part through. He frantically tried to come up with something. He thought about his house in Oregon, his bedroom, and the walls covered in first place ribbons from races he won as a kid.

"Blue Ribbon Sports," he boasted with as much confidence as he could gather.

The company accepted, and Phil's not even a real company (yet) was already the United States west coast distributor of Japan's largest shoe company.

Blue Ribbon Sports eventually became Nike. Phil saw an opportunity for himself to not be a cog in the machine, but to work on his own schedule. He was a Stanford M.B.A. graduate and could have taken any banking job imaginable, but he knew himself well enough to not do that.[143]

Obviously, creating Nike is a very entrepreneurial thing to do, and you may be questioning what this has to do with being a free agent. Many entrepreneurs started just working for themselves with no goals in sight, and there are some traits to Phil's story that we can link directly to being a free agent.

1. He didn't initially dream of having the largest sporting goods company in the world. He didn't make the shoes, and he didn't even want to. He wanted to work for himself and bring Japanese shoes to the States.
2. He used his creativity to look at the market differently. He saw an opportunity for a Japanese shoe in the United States and took advantage of that.
3. He knew the risks he was taking and accepted them. The opportunity cost wasn't extremely high. If he failed, it sets him back a couple of years on a traditional career path and could have cost him potential career growth. But he wasn't married, had no debt, and didn't have much to lose.

Free agents battle with many of the same questions that entrepreneurs deal with. What am I risking? Is there a market for my services? Do I have the skills to run my own business?

Entrepreneurship is about finding a problem that people have and creating a business to solve that problem. That is easily

---

143 Jack Meyer, "History of Nike: Timeline and Facts," TheStreet, August 14, 2019.

transferable to a free agent. Rather than having a product as a solution, as a freelancer, you personally are the solution in solving problems or filling gaps for a company.

The difference lies when we talk about the most exceptional entrepreneurs and the most outstanding free agents. The best entrepreneurs solve problems that people didn't even know they had. Henry Ford once said, "If I had asked people what they wanted, they would have said faster horses."[144]

The best free agents perform their services more efficiently, take on more or more significant clients, and continue to raise their prices. For a company to pay you to do a task, it's likely going to be a problem that a company knows it has and needs fixing. Either that or you are going to have to do some serious convincing.

The good news is you don't need to have a full-fledged business with multiple employees to solve problems for other companies. Sixty-two percent of small businesses don't even have any staff.[145] They are one-person shops. If they need something they can't do or don't have the time to, they'll contract it out. There is also no need to go get an office, either. Sixty percent of these solopreneurs are home-based.[146]

---

144 Deep Patel, "25 Quotes to Inspire Your Entrepreneurial Journey," Entrepreneur, April 23, 2017.

145 Dragomir Simovic, "39 Entrepreneur Statistics You Need to Know In 2020," SmallBizGenius, August 5, 2019.

146 Aleks Merkovich, "15 Entrepreneurship Statistics You Should Know," Fit Small Business, March 25, 2019.

As we've discussed, the world is becoming more welcoming to this type of worker in the business world.

At some point, it becomes about priorities for the individual. Can my family afford for me to take these risks? Can I get the healthcare I need at a price I can afford if I don't work for a traditional employer?

But there is more to it than having nothing else to lose. After all, eighty-three percent of self-employed individuals chose this as their desired career path.[147] That's a significant number of people, and many of them have a lot to lose; they just see self-employment as the best path.

FULL-TIME FREE AGENT

Some people just aren't made for the slow path and don't see the purpose of hedging their bet. It would create a more gradual transition, and a slow transition into anything may sound exhausting and surprisingly more challenging to pull off. Some people just want to jump into their new career structure, and that's okay too.

The full-time free agent is unique in many ways. The salesmanship, the constant networking, and overall hustle needed are not unlike the effort required to move up the corporate ladder. Regularly taking on new tasks and responsibilities, creating a personal brand as the go-to person, and doing

---

147 FreshBooks, "3rd Annual American Self-Employment Report: Fresh-Books Research," FreshBooks, 2019.

everything you can to make it happen are all similarities shared between a full-time free agent and a corporate prospect.

So, what does a full-time free agency really look like?

For some, it's a collection of side hustles all at one time. For others, it's a project that takes up their entire focus for a specified time.

Ask any full-time free agent, and they will tell you there is very little more comforting than having a longer-term contract, whether that be for a certain number of hours a week or a longer-term project. A contract means consistent money coming in.

If you're still working a full-time set of hours, and then having to continually find contracts and worry about downtimes, why not just take a traditional full-time job?

Flexibility.

Almost eighty percent of full-time freelancers say flexibility in their schedule (as in days/times they work) is a primary reason they are self-employed.[148] It gives you the chance to work when you are most productive and adjust your schedule accordingly.

---

148 "Freelancing in America: 2019," *Upwork/Freelancers Union*, LinkedIn SlideShare (September 23, 2019).

But the problem isn't becoming self-employed, there are fifteen million Americans that are full-time self-employed. The problem is staying that way.[149]

Taking that leap into self-employment will be a lonely activity. Being your own boss puts a lot of pressure on yourself to succeed and trust your business savviness. Ultimately, just over twenty-two percent of small businesses fail within the first year.[150]

It's the willingness to accept the uncertainty when you know there is a more comfortable, less stressful alternative. You just don't want that option.

So, what's really the motivation behind giving up all of those perks of being traditionally employed? Remember, these trends into self-employment were already happening before COVID-19, back when people weren't losing their jobs left and right, forcing many into gig work or self-employment.

It comes down to a lifestyle. A mindset. The "I want to work for myself" attitude that burns through so many people. The chance to work on your own terms.

Almost forty percent of self-employed say they work fewer hours but are actually more productive.[151] That better utiliza-

---

149 Dragomir Simovic, "39 Entrepreneur Statistics You Need to Know In 2020," SmallBizGenius, August 5, 2019.

150 Ibid.

151 FreshBooks, "3rd Annual American Self-Employment Report: FreshBooks Research," FreshBooks, 2019.

tion of time allows for more time with family, or to travel, or for more opportunities to push yourself out of your comfort zone.

We've now seen what entrepreneurship looks like to the highest degree, so let's see what we can learn from a person who started their freelance business without much preparation in mind.

FROM STARTUP TO FREELANCE

Paul had it great.

He was successfully leading a developing market out of Richmond, Virginia for a startup, King of Pops, a popsicle company that set out to bring "Unexpected Moments of Happiness" by having great flavors with great ingredients. Paul's task was to lead his region by developing and growing the brand.

And that he did. He led his market to the second-largest market in the country for King of Pops.

Entrepreneurship was a way for Paul to work for himself. Even though he was technically working for the founders, he controlled his market and loved being able to grow the business with his vision. King of Pops was on his mind 24/7, and his anxious personality drove him and his region to success.

But as the popsicle company became larger and larger, the business models for the different regions became more standardized with the direction given by headquarters.

Eventually, Paul found that he wasn't growing and learning the way he wanted to. So, he turned to freelancing.

He had graduated from the University of Georgia in 2007 with a bachelor's degree in business, and just like most college graduates at that time, finding a job became an almost impossible task.

So, he began his career as a Spanish teacher, knowing this was a temporary stop until the job market recovered.

About halfway through his second year of teaching, he approached some friends of his from college who had just started King of Pops. He felt that he was missing something, and teaching Spanish wasn't giving him the excitement he wanted in his everyday life.

Paul began by taking on many different roles. King of Pops became his passion, and marketing became his way to share it with his region. Because of this burning desire to grow the company, he found himself constantly working, and if he wasn't working, he was still thinking about ways to improve the business.

"We were all kind of figuring it out as we went, and that really appealed to me," Paul said when describing the early years of King of Pops.

Over time, things grew to be more comfortable, and every year got progressively better for him. He was learning, growing, and in charge of his career. It was precisely the career that he was looking for.

By year four, that started to change. Paul found himself working a lot less and getting as much, if not more, accomplished. Sounds terrible, right?

"I felt like I was not growing and didn't have any new challenges."

Over time, he began to realize that his personal growth goals were not going to be accomplished if he stayed in his current capacity. Because he had been through so many ups and so many downs with King of Pops, it wasn't easy for him to just leave. After all, he had put in so many hours and poured his heart into it; how could he just walk away?

Eventually, that burning desire to grow and get out of his comfort zone took over. He decided it was time to leave.

That left Paul with multiple options. Going to another startup could be exhilarating but could also leave him with less control of his work. Freelancing would give him control but adds risk when it comes to money and benefits.

Paul chose the latter and jumped in to become a full-time freelancer.

Unlike some others, Paul didn't have clients lined up already. He had been in charge of a region and still needed to determine what skills he could bring to other companies.

In doing a deep dive into what he enjoyed and found success doing during his time at King of Pops, he realized that digital marketing was something he could bring to the table. But, becoming a freelance digital marketer presented many new challenges.

"If I'm going to freelance, I have to have the skill of Facebook ads," said Paul as he began putting together necessities for his new personal business.

Even though he had significant experience doing much of this work, it wasn't formalized nor complete; however, once he decided to be a freelance digital marketer, he knew he had to go all in on it.

After leaving King of Pops, he started taking courses online and consuming as much information as he could about digital marketing. He then presented his ideas to his friends who owned their own businesses, asking if he could provide pro-bono work to build up his portfolio.

It hasn't all been perfect, but he appreciates the daily grind.

"I've had it where nothing might happen for four to six weeks in terms of new business coming in, but I'm working on existing client work, and if I'm not working, I'm putting out content."

Paul has been freelancing for more than a year as a digital marketer and has undoubtedly seen the ups and downs of being out on your own, specifically, the jumping in approach.

"All the mental growth and emotional intelligence that I have from those difficult times where I had years of nothing but stress and anxiety have helped me deal with the lows of freelancing."

Paul admits to the toll that beginning your freelancing journey has on a person. His experience working in a startup put him in a state of mind that was comfortable with uncertainty and has led him to deal with the emotional rollercoaster that freelancing can be.

That's the price you pay for freedom. You get to set your own goals and priorities, but most importantly, get to decide why you're in business.

We see the similarities between Phil and Paul and the mindsets they had when deciding to work for themselves. Phil knew he didn't have much to lose and knew the typical route wasn't for him. Paul chose a path of uncertainty, and after his experiences in living a more entrepreneurial lifestyle already, he was very comfortable with the risk.

The "free" life had given him the confidence he needed to feel good about succeeding. He also knew what the skill he would take to the freelancing market would be. He made sure to narrow focus on his craft and continue to learn.

Assessing your career and the stage you are currently at will be a critical element of deciding how you want to approach a free agent lifestyle. If you're like Morgan from the previous chapter and you still feel that you have many more experiences to gain, earn the income and push off being a full-time free agent.

If you think you are ready to jump in, make sure you understand what you are getting into. Both Phil and Paul show that being comfortable with uncertainty is truly a must. Once you are ready to go, buckle up and get prepared for the ups and downs of the rollercoaster known as a full-time free agent.

FINAL THOUGHTS

—

*"Many of life's failures are people who
did not realize how close they were
to success when they gave up."*

— THOMAS EDISON

I began the journey of writing this book in October of 2019,
months before COVID-19 ravaged through the world.

With over forty million Americans filing for unemployment,
will it finally make us rethink the employer-employee relationship and how benefits are given out?[152] Maybe it's time
to rethink if a W-2 should be the only type of employment
in America. Here are the questions I have:

---

152 Anneken Tappe, "1 In 4 American Workers Have Filed for Unemployment
Benefits during the Pandemic," CNN May 28, 2020.

Do people really have to form a business, even as an individual, to qualify for some of the benefits a traditional employee receives?

Could we still allow companies to contribute to people's retirement and overall well-being as a reward for the work *completed* for the company, instead of only when they *work for* the company?

The coronavirus pandemic has also brought to everyone's attention the growing need to be flexible in not only where you work, but also how you work and what you are working on.

As we've discussed throughout the entire book, the system as it stands right now is not set up for free agents. That's why they are contrarians. They are going against the grain of what is traditional.

Many books, blogs, articles, social media groups, etc., are incredible resources for free agents and those looking to become free agents. However, there are a few things they tend to lack.

Thirty-six percent of freelancers want additional training to improve their skills in starting and growing a freelance business.[153]

---

153 "Freelancing in America: 2019," *Upwork/Freelancers Union*, LinkedIn SlideShare (September 23, 2019).

Have you ever searched the web for "getting started as a free-lancer" or "how to become my own boss?" It comes back with limited useful results to getting started.

Many of the results sound a lot like people telling you *how to grow your freelance business* or maybe *how to find your passion and make it a career.*

What if we already know what we want to do? Or we don't need to worry about growing the business because there is no business yet. I've spent the last year talking to freelancers, independent contractors, solopreneurs, and everyone associated with free agents, and many of them shared similar frustrations.

Getting started.

"Get a good CPA, create an LLC, file as an S Corp."

"What?" That was my initial response to all of the advice out there. "How do I even go about doing that?"

It seemed as though I needed to create an LLC. How do you do that? Logically, I spent hours researching online lawyers and was completely overwhelmed. Don't get me wrong, they made it look really easy, but did I really have to spend a couple extra hundred dollars and another eighty dollars a year to maintain some lawyer relationship that I wasn't convinced I needed?

No, I didn't.

Luckily, my uncle, Todd Manns, a man who never has an opinion he doesn't share and first hired me on as an independent contractor, talked some sense into me. He had started out as a free agent ten years ago and told me this about paying for a registered agent.

"It's all bullshit."

Now, neither of us are lawyers, and of course, you should consult with one if you feel like you need one, but it drives home the deeper point. Free agents need mentors or coaches, especially in the early days of getting started.

That's why my partner Christian Lagarde and I founded Be Your Own Boss, LLC. Through all of our research and interviews, we found that people needed coaching, especially at the early stages of their free agent career. We are curating courses and articles that will bring the information you need directly to you in an easy to understand format. Check it out at www.thebyoboss.com.

I want to thank you for taking the time to read this book. I hope you've found it insightful, interesting, and maybe even entertaining. Free agents are going to play a very significant part in the future of work, and I hope that this book helped open some eyes to a world that you may not have noticed.

If you do decide to go work for yourself, I wish you the best of luck. If you don't, get ready for the future of work, because it's coming.

NEXT STEPS

If you know you are wanting to start your own business using your skills as its product but don't know where to start, here is a progression you can use to become a free agent.

1. **Map out your skills.**

- It's time to take an honest look at your background. What are you good at? What skills do you have that are currently in demand? Go through your background and look for skills that are easily transferable and are traits that separate you from others.
- This self-evaluation isn't always easy, but it's critical to understanding your potential value to organizations. Just know, at this point, you may suffer from what's known as "imposter syndrome." Don't worry; every free agent has had that feeling before. You have the skills and are capable of being on your own.

2. Find the demand.

- Post on social media that you are taking on clients and list the service you are looking to provide.
- Go through LinkedIn jobs, Upwork, Fiverr, Catalant, etc., and compare yourself to the profiles you see, finding your points of differentiation.
- If you are sure you want to leave, talk to your company about changing the structure of your work. Many free agents have contracts with former employers.

3. Measure your personal situation.

- What do your finances look like? Do you have built-up savings that you can pull from if things are slower than expected? Maintaining an adequate emergency fund while you're self-employed keeps you from being forced to take on lower contracts in the name of "getting by for now."
- What does your family situation look like? Are you married, and does your spouse have benefits like healthcare that you can obtain? How does your income fit together? Do you have major upcoming expenses or kids going to college soon? All are things to consider, not things to prevent you from going out on your own full-time.

4. Decide how you want to enter.

- Is this going to be the new normal for you, something you want to do part-time ,or just done in the interim? If it is intended to be interim for you, it's important to understand what you need to get out of it.

- Take into account health insurance, retirement benefits, and your spouse's situation. Do you have any savings to help over the next few months and just need a little bit to tide you over, or do you need to replace your full salary?

5. **Find your ideal client.**

- Do you have a client that looks like you'll be able to do a significant amount of work for? You don't have to have this type of client now, or even ever, but it makes your life easier if you do.
- Learn what they need to hire people for and how you can fit into their plans. If they don't need you for anything, are there similar companies that could? Tailor how you are branding yourself for the audience you are trying to reach.

6. **Build your business.**

- At this point, you know just how serious you are about doing this. You may soon find out that many companies will want you to have business insurance, and you should consider creating an LLC or a separate entity for your business. This might be a good time to check in with a CPA and/or a lawyer. Better yet, find a coach or mentor to learn about what they did, then go check-in.
- Create your website, make business cards, and prepare your home office. You are a business now, and would you really trust a business without a website? It doesn't need to be fancy but it should have on there with the info you want a potential client to see about you.
- Open a business checking account. Find one that is convenient, easy to use, and has people who understand how

the account works. If the COVID-19 response and PPP loans showed us anything, the bank you choose matters.

7. **Create your pitch.**

- What makes your business unique? If you were to meet a hiring manager tomorrow and you had to describe what your freelancing business is, you better be able to explain it and sound confident in doing so. Part of that comes from experience in the field; the other part comes from clearly mapping out what your business is going to be.
- Freelancing is personal branding on steroids, and branding has never been more important for you than it's about to be. Get your pitch ready. Practice it, and perfect it.

8. **Find your differentiation.**

- Look for potential partnerships. Do you have a former colleague that has skills that compliment you? Have you connected with other individuals who know what you bring to the table? Businesses want creative problem solvers; finding ways to fill your personal gaps is just the beginning.
- Just like you should do when writing your resume, tailor your bio and skill set to the jobs you are looking for, What skills or accomplishments that may not have been part of your primary job make you a perfect match for the type of work you are seeking? Are there other skills you can quickly learn that you are seeing employers are searching for?

9. **Hustle.**

- This may seem obvious, but finding temporary and contract work is not simple, and there isn't a perfect formula. Scrolling through Upwork, Fiverr, or announcing to your network that you are accepting contract work doesn't take much effort. Reaching out to companies and hiring managers does. The good news is, you aren't asking for a full-time job that pays benefits, and that is much less threatening in the eyes of a recruiter.
- Remember why you are going out on this venture. If you are still looking for a job that fits in with your career and you just need to pay some bills in the meantime, know that and find the gig that makes that goal achievable. Who knows, you might just find that working for yourself is just what you've been missing. If this is the new normal, create a process that works for you.

ACKNOWLEDGMENTS

——

Without the 26 years of jokes at my expense from my friends and family, I would never have the courage to put my own work on Amazon and wait for the negative reviews to come pouring in.

I first must say thank you to the free agents who allowed me to share their stories with you, without their generosity this book would never have happened. In order where they appear in the book: Jennifer Bowman, Vanessa Ferragut, Holly Harper, Morgan Mendez, Joshua Wilson, Stefanie O'Connell Rodriguez, April Palmer, Dante Atkins, Kim Barbano, Morgan Rogers, and Paul Cassimuss. I also want to thank Kristen Anderson from Catch.co for sharing her perspective with me.

Writing this book was the most grueling and difficult thing I've done in my life up to this point. None of it would happen without Eric Koester convincing me to challenge myself. I also needed every bit of help from New Degree Press and am extremely appreciative of my editors Stephanie McKibben and Al Bagdonas.

Most of all, I want to thank those who lent their support for this exciting project :

My family: Jessica Nielsen and our dog Otto, Mom, Dad, Carl, & Todd. My grandparents: Bruce & Nancy Jones and Arvey & Phyllis Arnold. Todd & Steph Manns, Tyler & Jenn Manns, Michael Jones and Nick Barsody.

The Georgetown community: Amanda Kosty, Anna Glazkova, Anya Bowen & Isaac Fradin, Becky Davidson, Charlie Stack, Danny Solow, Doreen Amorosa, Jupiter El-Asmar, Larry Verbiest, Michael Kuebler, Montek Singh, and Rishi Malhotra, with a special shout out to Ben Wrobel & Chelsea Geyer for all the work you've put into this with me.

I've been lucky enough to have many lifelong friends, former colleagues and classmates that I also want to thank for their continued support: Andrew Willard, Brody Northcott, Christian Bacio, Christian Lagarde, Cortland Randolph, Evan Flatto, Inga Avila, Jillian Fehringer, Eric & Lauren Nielsen, Phil & Julie Nielsen, Lexis Taylor, Lisbel Woods, Mandy Tate, Meryl Hooten, Michael Piersanti, Michael-Anne Goodart, Nicolette Johnson, Renee Lu & Tom Nagy, Ryan Bernard, Tammie & Shawn O'Brien, Teresa & Dave Taylor, and my high school baseball coach, Tory Humphrey.

REFERENCES

———

INTRODUCTION:

"Freelancing in America: 2017." *Upwork/Freelancers Union*. LinkedIn SlideShare (September 2017). https://www.slideshare.net/upwork/freelancing-in-america-2017/1.

"Freelancing in America: 2019." *Upwork/Freelancers Union*. LinkedIn SlideShare (September 23, 2019). https://www.slideshare.net/upwork/freelancing-in-america-2019/1.

CHAPTER 1: RISK & THE GIG ECONOMY

Coombes, Andrea. "Millennials Are Good at Saving, But Investing? Not So Much." *Forbes*. March 13, 2018.https://www.forbes.com/sites/andreacoombes/2018/03/13/millennials-are-good-at-saving-but-investing-not-so-much/#30e8e4237266.

"Freelancing in America: 2019." *Upwork/Freelancers Union*. LinkedIn SlideShare (September 23, 2019). https://www.slideshare.net/upwork/freelancing-in-america-2019/1.

Harley, Aurora. "Prospect Theory and Loss Aversion: How Users Make Decisions." *Nielsen Norman Group.* June 19, 2016. https://www.nngroup.com/articles/prospect-theory/.

Kahneman, Daniel *Thinking, Fast and Slow.* New York: Farrar, Straus and Giroux, 2013, 280.

Manyika, James., Lund, Susan., Bughin, Jacques., Robinson, Kelsey., Mischke, Jan. Mahajan, Deepa. "Independent Work: Choice, Necessity, and the Gig Economy." *McKinsey & Company.* October 2016. https://www.mckinsey.com/featured-insights/employment-and-growth/independent-work- choice-necessity-and-the-gig-economy.

Merriam-Webster.com Dictionary, s.v. "gig economy," accessed June 6, 2020, https://www.merriam-webster.com/dictionary/gig%20economy.

Moreno, Johan. "Google Follows A Growing Workplace Trend: Hiring More Contractors Than Employees." *Forbes.* May 31, 2019. https://www.forbes.com/sites/johanmoreno/2019/05/31/goo-gle-follows- a-growing-workplace-trend-hiring-more-contrac-tors-than-employees/#33fb9b26447f.

Selby-Green, Michael. "The Gig Economy Is Coming for Your Office Job - Here's How It Works for Companies Doing It Already." *Business Insider.* May 28, 2018. https://www.businessinsider.com/gig-economy-set-to-hit-the-office-2018-5.

Robinson, Ryan. "60 Entrepreneurs Share Best Business Advice & Success Tips." *RyRob.com* (blog). February 6, 2https://www.ryrob.com/start-business-advice/.

Rosenfeld, Michael J., Thomas, Reuben J., and Hausen, Sonia. "Disintermediating Your Friends: How Online Dating in the United States Displaces Other Ways of Meeting." *Proceedings of the National Academy of Sciences*. August 20, 2019. 17753-17758. https://doi.org/1908630116.

CHAPTER 2: THE OPPORTUNITY

Jarvis, Chase. "How to Find Your Creative Calling." Interview by Kevin Rose. *The Kevin Rose Show*. Podcast Notes. September 22, 2019. https://podcastnotes.org/kevin-rose-show/jarvis/.

"Freelancing in America: 2019." *Upwork/Freelancers Union*. LinkedIn SlideShare (September 23, 2019). https://www.slideshare.net/upwork/freelancing-in-america-2019/1.

Marks, Gene. "Monster Poll: 76 Percent of Job Seekers Say Their Boss Is 'Toxic'." *Inc Magazine*. October 18, 2018. https://www.inc.com/gene-marks/monster-poll-76-percent-of-job-seekers-say-their-boss-is-toxic.html.

McPherson, Susan. "Corporate Responsibility: What to Expect In 2019." *Forbes*. January 16, 2019. https://www.forbes.com/sites/susanmcpherson/2019/01/14/corporate-responsibility-what-to-expect-in-2019/#61d35dae690f.

Mobbs, Carole Hallett. "The Trailing Spouse and Identity." *Expat Child* (blog). January 4, 2017. https://expatchild.com/trailing-spouse-identity/.

Staff Report. "Why You Need Workforce Planning." *workforce. com*. October 24, 2002. https://www.workforce.com/news/why-you-need-workforce-planning.

The Council of Economic Advisors. "Military Spouses in the Labor Market." *The White House*. May 2018. https://www.whitehouse.gov/wp-content/uploads/2018/05/Military-Spouses-in-the-Labor- Market.pdf.

"The White-Collar Gig Economy." *Mavenlink*. Mavenlink. Accessed on May 14, 2020. https://go.mavenlink.com/hubfs/Downloadable_Content/Ebooks_And_White_Papers/white-collar-gig- economy-on-demand-trends-oct-2017.pdf?submissionGuid=0dfe4d54-0081 -4268-9407-db4d64312999.

"Future Workforce 2019: How Younger Generations Are Reshaping the Future." *Upwork/Inavero*. LinkedIn SlideShare. March 5, 2019. https://www.slideshare.net/upwork/future-workforce-2019-how-younger- generations-are-reshaping-the-future-workforce.

CHAPTER 3: TECHNOLOGY & THE CHANGING WORKPLACE

Airtasker. "The Benefits of Working from Home." *Airtasker Blog*, March 31, 2020. https://www.airtasker.com/blog/the-benefits-of-working-from-home/.

Crane, Daniel A., "Antitrust's Unconventional Politics" (2018). *Law & Economics Working Papers*. 153. https://repository.law.umich.edu/law_econ_current/153.

Manyika, James., Lund, Susan., Chui, Michael., Bughin, Jacques., Woetzel, Jonathan., Batra, Parul., Ko, Ryan., Sanghvi, Sarabh. November 28, 2017. https://www.mckinsey.com/featured-insights/future-of-work/jobs-lost-jobs-gained-what-the-future-of-work-will-mean-for-jobs-skills-and-wages.

De León, Riley. "Coronavirus Reopening: How Companies Including Facebook, Tesla and Mastercard Are Bringing Workers Back." *CNBC*. CNBC. May 26, 2020. https://www.cnbc.com/2020/05/26/companies-reopening-coronavirus-live-updates.html.

Desoutter Tools. "Industrial Revolution - From Industry 1.0 to Industry 4.0." *Desoutter Industrial Tools*. Desoutter Tools. Accessed May 3, 2020. https://www.desouttertools.com/industry-4-0/news/503/industrial-revolution-from-industry-1-0-to-industry-4-0.

Eisen, Ben. "Workers Are Fleeing Big Cities for Smaller Ones and Taking Their Jobs with Them." *The Wall Street Journal. Dow Jones & Company*. September 7, 2019. https://www.wsj.com/articles/workers-are-fleeing-big-cities-for-small-onesand-taking-their-jobs-with-them-11567848600.

"Freelancing in America: 2019." *Upwork/Freelancers Union*. LinkedIn SlideShare (September 23, 2019). https://www.slideshare.net/upwork/freelancing-in-america-2019/1.

History.com Editors, "Industrial Revolution," History.com. *A&E Television Networks*. October 29, 2009. https://www.history.com/topics/industrial-revolution/industrial-revolution.

Houston, John., Kester, Boy. "Talent Analytics in Practice." *Deloitte Insights*, March 8, 2014. https://www2.deloitte.com/us/en/insights/focus/human-capital-trends/2014/hc-trends-2014-talent-analytics.html.

Hovenkamp, Herbert., Kovacic, William., and Bhargava, Hemant. "Why Breaking Up Big Tech Could Do More Harm Than Good." *Knowledge@Wharton*. March 26, 2019. https://knowledge.wharton.upenn.edu/article/why-breaking-up-big-tech-could-do-more-harm-than-good/.

Kolbjørnsrud, Vegard., Amico, Richard., Thomas, Robert J. "How Artificial Intelligence Will Redefine Management." *Harvard Business Review*. November 2, 2016. https://hbr.org/2016/11/how-artificial -intelligence-will-redefine-management.

Lewis, Michael. *Moneyball: The Art of Winning an Unfair Game.* New York, NY: W.W. Norton, 2004.

Longman, Phillip. "Why the Economic Fates of America's Cities Diverged." *The Atlantic*. November 28, 2015. https://www.theatlantic.com/business/archive/2015/11/cities-economic-fates-diverge/417372/.

Manne, Kevin. "How Artificial Intelligence Will Impact Self-Employment." *Phys.org*. October 1, 2019. https://phys.org/news/2019-10-artificial-intelligence-impact-self-employment.html.

Matt McFarland. "How Google Is Making Sure Cows Won't Foil Its Self-Driving Cars." *The Washington Post*. April 7, 2015. https://www.washingtonpost.com/news/innovations/wp/2015/04/07/

how-google-is-making-sure-cows-wont-foil-its-self-driving-cars/?arc404=true.

Merriam-Webster.com *Dictionary*, s.v. "artificial intelligence." Accessed June 2, 2020. https://www.merriam-webster.com/dictionary/artificial%20intelligence.

Merriam-Webster.com *Dictionary*, s.v. "machine learning." Accessed June 2, 2020. https://www.merriam-webster.com/dictionary/machine%20learning.

"The Work of the Future: Shaping Technology and Institutions." *MIT Work of the Future*. 2019.

Muro, Mark., Whiton, Jacob., Maxim, Robert. "What Jobs Are Affected by AI? Better-Paid, Better-Educated Workers Face the Most Exposure." *Brookings*. November 20, 2019. https://www.brookings.edu/research/what-jobs-are-affected-by-ai-better-paid-better-educated-workers-face-the-most-exposure/.

Niiler, Eric. "How the Second Industrial Revolution Changed Americans' Lives." *History.com*. A&E Television Networks. January 25, 2019. https://www.history.com/news/second-industrial-revolution-advances.

Smith, Chris., McGuire, Brian., Huang, Ting., Yang, Gary. "The History of Artificial Intelligence." *History of Computing*. University of Washington, December 2006. https://courses.cs.washington.edu/courses/csep590/06au/projects/history-ai.pdf.

Strutz, Martin. "Freelancers and Technology Are Leading the Workforce Revolution." *Forbes*. November 17, 2016. https://www.

forbes.com/sites/berlinschoolofcreativeleadership/2016/11/10/
free-lancers-and-technology-are-leading-the-workforce-revolu-
tion/#460a203b5d21.

"Tulsa Remote." Tulsa Remote. Accessed May 4, 2020. https://tul-
saremote.com/.

U.S. Bureau of Economic Analysis, Per Capita Personal Income in
New York-Newark-Jersey City, NY-NJ-PA (MSA) [NEWY636PCPI],
retrieved from FRED, Federal Reserve Bank of St. Louis; https://
fred.stlouisfed.org/series/NEWY636PCPI, May 3, 2020.

U.S. Bureau of Economic Analysis, Per Capita Personal Income in
St. Louis, MO-IL (MSA) [STLPCPI], retrieved from FRED, Fed-
eral Reserve Bank of St. Louis; https://fred.stlouisfed.org/series/
STLPCPI, May 3, 2020.

Wright, Ryan. "Moneyball: A Look Inside Major League Baseball
and the Oakland A's." *Bleacher Report.* Bleacher Report, September
20, 2011. https://bleacherreport.com/articles/858470-moneyball-a-
look-inside-major-league-baseball-and-the-oakland-as.

CHAPTER 4: GOVERNMENT'S ROLE IN THE FUTURE OF WORK

Barney, Lee, "Majority of Today's Retirees Have a Pension," *PLA-
NADVISER* (blog). September 26, 2016. https://www.planadviser.
com/majority-of-todays-retirees-have-a-pension/.

Crane, Daniel A."Antitrust's Unconventional Politics." *Law & Economics Working Papers.* 2018. 153. https://repository.law.umich.edu/
law_econ_current/153.

De León, Riley. "Coronavirus Reopening: How Companies Including Facebook, Tesla and Mastercard Are Bringing Workers Back." *CNBC*. CNBC, May 26, 2020. https://www.cnbc.com/2020/05/26/companies-reopening-coronavirus-live-updates.html.

Eisen, Ben. "Workers Are Fleeing Big Cities for Smaller Ones-and Taking Their Jobs with Them." *The Wall Street Journal. Dow Jones & Company*. September 7, 2019. https://www.wsj.com/articles/workers-are-fleeing-big-cities-for-small-onesand-taking-their-jobs-with-them-11567848600.

"Research Report: The Freelance Political Perspective Report." *Fiverr*. (October 2018). http://www.freelance-perspectives.fiverr.com/Fiverr_v2a.pdf.

"Freelancing in America: 2019." *Upwork/Freelancers Union*. LinkedIn SlideShare (September 23, 2019). https://www.slideshare.net/upwork/freelancing-in-america-2019/1.

Upwork/Freelancers Union, "Freelancing in America: 2017," LinkedIn SlideShare, September 2017. https://www.slideshare.net/upwork/freelancing-in-america-2017/1.

"High Deductible Health Plans: What Are the Pros and Cons?." *Knowledge@Wharton*. Wharton. June 17, 2019. https://knowledge.wharton.upenn.edu/article/high-deductible-health-plans-pros-and-cons/.

Hovenkamp, Herbert., Kovacic, William., Bhargav, Hemant. "Why Breaking Up Big Tech Could Do More Harm Than Good." *Knowledge@Wharton*. March 26, 2019. https://knowledge.wharton.upenn.

edu/article/why-breaking-up-big-tech-could-do-more-harm-than-good/.

Longman, Phillip. "Why the Economic Fates of America's Cities Diverged." *The Atlantic*. November 28, 2015. https://www.theatlantic.com/business/archive/2015/11/cities-economic-fates-diverge/417372/.

Mishel, Lawrence. "Uber and the Labor Market: Uber Drivers' Compensation, Wages, and the Scale of Uber and the Gig Economy." *Economic Policy Institute*. May 15, 2018. https://www.epi.org/publication/uber-and-the-labor-market-uber-drivers-compensation-wages-and-the-scale-of-uber-and-the-gig-economy/.

NBC. "Uber, Lyft Driver Protest Brings Manhattan Traffic to Nearly Total Stop at Rush Hour." *NBC New York*. NBC New York. September 17, 2019. https://www.nbcnewyork.com/news/local/uber-lyft-driver-protest-brings-manhattan-traffic-to-nearly-dead-stop-at-rush-hour/1991331/.

Strutz, Martin. "Freelancers and Technology Are Leading the Workforce Revolution." *Forbes*. November 17, 2016. https://www.forbes.com/sites/berlinschoolofcreativeleadership/2016/11/10/free-lancers-and-technology-are-leading-the-workforce-revolution/#460a203b5d21.

"The Independent Workforce: Sizing the Market in the United States." Fiverr, 2019. https://npm-assets.fiverrcdn.com/assets/@fiverr-private/freelance_impact/freelance-economy-2019.43a21dc.pdf.

Tappe, Anneken. "1 In 4 American Workers Have Filed for Unemployment Benefits during the Pandemic," *CNN*. May 28, 2020.

https://www.cnn.com/2020/05/28/economy/unemployment-benefits-coronavirus/index.html)

"Tulsa Remote." Tulsa Remote. Accessed May 4, 2020. https://tulsaremote.com/.

U.S. Bureau of Economic Analysis, Per Capita Personal Income in New York-Newark-Jersey City, NY-NJ-PA (MSA) [NEWY636PCPI], retrieved from FRED, Federal Reserve Bank of St. Louis; https://fred.stlouisfed.org/series/NEWY636PCPI, May 3, 2020

U.S. Bureau of Economic Analysis, Per Capita Personal Income in St. Louis, MO-IL (MSA) [STLPCPI], retrieved from FRED, Federal Reserve Bank of St. Louis; https://fred.stlouisfed.org/series/STLPCPI, May 3, 2020.

"Employee Tenure Summary." *U.S. Bureau of Labor Statistics.* U.S. Department of Labor. September 20, 2018. https://www.bls.gov/news.release/tenure.nro.htm.

Yurieff, Kaya. "Everything We Know about Amazon's HQ2 Search." *CNN.* November 5, 2018. https://www.cnn.com/2018/11/05/tech/amazon-hq2-update/index.html.

CHAPTER 5: BRING YOUR PASSION, DON'T FOLLOW IT

Brand Building Through Storytelling. "Molly Bloom - Poker Entrepreneur - Keynote Speaker - Summit 2018." June 4, 2018. https://www.youtube.com/watch?v=Ze4oCumNHSA.

Bloom, Molly. *Molly's Game: The True Story of the 26-Year-Old Woman behind the Most Exclusive, High-Stakes Underground Poker Game in the World.* New York, NY: Dey Street Books, 2017.

"Company Information." Starbucks Coffee Company. Accessed May 15, 2020. https://www.starbucks.com/about-us/company-information.

Deloitte. "Deloitte Study: Only 13 Percent of the US Workforce Is Passionate About Their Jobs." *PR Newswire*: June 26, 2018. https://www.prnewswire.com/news-releases/deloitte-study-only-13-percent-of-the-us-workforce-is-passionate-about-their-jobs-300469952.html.

Kerpen, Dave. "15 Things You Need to Know About Passion." *Inc.* March 27, 2014. https://www.inc.com/dave-kerpen/15-quotes-on-passion-to-inspire-a-better-life.html.

O'Keefe, Paul A., Dweck, Carol S., Walton Gregory M. "Implicit Theories of Interest: Finding Your Passion or Developing It?" *Psychological Science.* 2018. http://gregorywalton-stanford.weebly.com/uploads/4/9/4/4/49448111/okeefedweckwalton_2018.pdf.

Rowe, Mike. "'Dirty Jobs' Host Mike Rowe: Here's Why You Should Never Follow Your Passion." Interview by Bryan Elliot. *Behind the Brand.* Business Insider, December 11, 2014. https://www.businessinsider.com/mike-rowe-freelancing-career-passion-2014-12.

Team, Glassdoor. "New Survey: Company Mission & Culture Matter More Than Salary: Glassdoor." *Glassdoor* (blog). July 10, 2019. https://www.glassdoor.com/blog/mission-culture-survey/.

CHAPTER 6: BE CREATIVE & THINK DIFFERENTLY

Armstrong, Jennifer Keishin. *Seinfeldia: How a Show About Nothing Changed Everything.* New York, NY: Simon & Schuster Paperbacks, an imprint of Simon & Schuster, Inc., 2017.

TED, "Luc de Brabandere: Reinventing Creative Thinking," June 2015. Video, 14:00. https://www.ted.com/talks/luc_de_brabandere_reinventing_creative_thinking.

Curtin, Melanie. "33 Quotes for Entrepreneurs That Will Uplift and Inspire." Inc.com. Inc., July 24, 2018. https://www.inc.com/melanie-curtin/33-inspirational-quotes-for-entrepreneurs.html.

Grant, Adam. *Originals: How Non-Conformists Move the World.* New York, NY. Penguin Books. 2017.7.

"Freelancing in America: 2019." *Upwork/Freelancers Union.* LinkedIn SlideShare (September 23, 2019). https://www.slideshare.net/upwork/freelancing-in-america-2019/1.

"Indian Summer." *Mad Men.* USA, October 4, 2007.

Naiman, Linda. "3 Keys to Finding a Creative Breakthrough." *Creativity at Work* (blog). October 21, 2019. https://www.creativityat-work.com/2019/10/21/3-keys-to-finding-a-creative-breakthrough/.

Catmull, Ed, and Wallace, Amy. *Creativity, Inc.: Overcoming the Unseen Forces That Stand in the Way of True Inspiration.* New York, NY. Random House, 2014. 1.

CHAPTER 7: YOU ARE THE BRAND

Godin, Seth. "The Freelancer and the Entrepreneur." *Medium*. June 5, 2016. https://medium.com/swlh/the-freelancer-and-the-entrepreneur-c79d2bbb52b2.

Godin, Seth. "The Simple First Rule of Branding and Marketing Anything (Even Yourself)." Seth's Blog (blog). December 17, 2011. https://seths.blog/2011/12/the-simple-first-rule-of-branding-and-marketing-anything-even-yourself.

Kim, Larry. "22 Inspiring Billionaire Quotes About Successful Personal Branding." *Inc.* July 15, 2015. https://www.inc.com/larry-kim/22-inspiring-billionaire-quotes-about-successful-personal-branding.html.

Luenendonk, Martin. "The Ultimate Career Choice: Generalist vs. Specialist." *Cleverism* (blog). March 23, 2016. https://www.cleverism.com/ultimate-career-choice-generalist-vs-specialist/.

CHAPTER 8: UNDERSTANDING YOURSELF

Airtasker. "The Benefits of Working from Home." *Airtasker Blog*, March 31, 2020. https://www.airtasker.com/blog/the-benefits-of-working-from-home/.

Merriam-Webster.com Dictionary, s.v. "bet," accessed June 6, 2020, https://www.merriam-webster.com/dictionary/bet.

"Confronting the Money Taboo." *Capital Group*. December 2018. https://www.capitalgroup.com/content/dam/cgc/shared-content/documents/reports/MFGEWP-062-1218O.pdf.

Duke, Annie. *Thinking in Bets: Making Smarter Decisions When You Don't Have All the Facts*. NY, NY. Portfolio/Penguin. 2019.

Edleson, Harriet. "Boomers Want to Work, Transition to Retirement." *AARP*. April 3, 2019. https://www.aarp.org/retirement/planning-for-retirement/info-2019/work-transition-survey.html.

"Freelancing in America: 2019." *Upwork/Freelancers Union*. LinkedIn SlideShare (September 23, 2019). https://www.slideshare.net/upwork/freelancing-in-america-2019/1.

Gough, Christina. "Number of Super Bowl Viewers (TV) 2019." *Statista*. February 10, 2020. https://www.statista.com/statistics/216526/super-bowl-us-tv-viewership/.

"How to Ask for A Raise." *PayScale*. Accessed May 9, 2020. https://www.payscale.com/data/how-to-ask-for-a-raise.

Jarvis, Paul. *Company of One: Why Staying Small Is the next Big Thing for Business*. Boston, MA. Mariner Books, Houghton Mifflin Harcourt. 2020.

Mansfield, Matt. "STARTUP STATISTICS - The Numbers You Need to Know." Small Business Trends. March 28, 2019. https://smallbiztrends.com/2019/03/startup-statistics-small-business.html.

Maske, Mark. "'Worst Play-Call in Super Bowl History' Will Forever Alter Perception of Seahawks, Patriots." *The Washington Post*. February 2, 2015. https://www.washingtonpost.com/news/sports/wp/2015/02/02/worst-play-call-in-super-bowl-history-will-forever-alter-perception-of-seahawks-patriots/.

Pofeldt, Elaine. "Want to Keep Your Business Small? Paul Jarvis Is Your Man." *Forbes.* January 17, 2019. https://www.forbes.com/sites/elainepofeldt/2019/01/17/want-to-keep-your-business-small-paul-jarvis-is-your-man/#1fe29fe66917.

"Study Explores Professional Mentor-Mentee Relationships in 2019," Olivet Nazarene University. 2019. https://online.olivet.edu/research-statistics-on-professional-mentors.

"The 2018 Fidelity Investments Couples & Money Study." *Fidelity Investments*, 2018. https://www.fidelity.com/bin-public/060_www_fidelity_com/documents/pr/couples-fact-sheet.pdf.

The Minimalists Podcast, and Paul Jarvis. "www.theminimalists.com." *www.theminimalists.com.* The Minimalists, July 15, 2019. https://www.youtube.com/watch?v=SzUSQcEpdoU.

US Census Bureau. "Average One-Way Commuting Time by Metropolitan Areas." The United States Census Bureau. United States Census Bureau, December 7, 2017. https://www.census.gov/library/visualizations/interactive/travel-time.html.

"With a 52-Card Deck, What Are the Odds of Drawing a Pair of Jacks?" *Wizard of Odds* (blog). Accessed May 11, 2020. https://wizardofodds.com/ask-the-wizard/texas-hold-em/probability-pairs/.

CHAPTER 9: HEDGE YOUR BET

Ferris, Timothy. *Tribe of Mentors: Short Life Advice from the Best in the World.* Boston. Houghton Mifflin Harcourt Publishing Company. 2018. 24.

"Freelancing in America: 2019." *Upwork/Freelancers Union*. Linke-dIn SlideShare (September 23, 2019). https://www.slideshare.net/ upwork/freelancing-in-america-2019/1.

"Live Episode! New Belgium Brewing Company: Kim Jordan." *How I Built This with Guy Raz*. NPR. September 10, 2018. https://www. npr.org/2018/09/07/645620049/live-episode-new-belgium-brew-ing-company-kim-jordan.

Loper, Nick. *The Side Hustle: How to Turn Your Spare Time into $1000 a Month or More*. March 3, 2015. Independently published

"National Beer Sales & Production Data." *Brewers Association*. Accessed May 12, 2020. https://www.brewersassociation.org/sta-tistics-and-data/national-beer-stats/.

"The Hartford's 2018 Side Business Survey." *The Hartford*. (Septem-ber 2018). https://mms.businesswire.com/media/20180925005605/ en/680213/1/TheHartford_Side_Business_Survey_InfographicFI-NAL.pdf.

CHAPTER 10: JUMPING IN

"Freelancing in America: 2019." *Upwork/Freelancers Union*. Linke-dIn SlideShare (September 23, 2019). https://www.slideshare.net/ upwork/freelancing-in-america-2019/1.

FreshBooks. "3rd Annual American Self-Employment Report: FreshBooks Research." *FreshBooks*. 2019. https://www.freshbooks. com/press/annualreport.

Knight, Phil. *Shoe Dog*. New York, NY. Scribner. 2016.

Merkovich, Aleks. "15 Entrepreneurship Statistics You Should Know." *Fit Small Business*. March 25, 2019. https://fitsmallbusiness.com/entrepreneurship-statistics/.

Meyer, Jack. "History of Nike: Timeline and Facts." *TheStreet*. August 14, 2019. https://www.thestreet.com/lifestyle/history-of-nike-15057083.

Simovic, Dragomir. "39 Entrepreneur Statistics You Need to Know In 2020." *SmallBizGenius*. August 5, 2019. https://www.smallbizgenius.net/by-the-numbers/entrepreneur-statistics/#gref.

FINAL THOUGHTS

"Freelancing in America: 2019." *Upwork/Freelancers Union*. LinkedIn SlideShare (September 23, 2019). https://www.slideshare.net/upwork/freelancing-in-america-2019/1.

"Home." Johns Hopkins Coronavirus Resource Center. Accessed May 24, 2020. https://coronavirus.jhu.edu/.

Tappe, Anneken. "1 In 4 American Workers Have Filed for Unemployment Benefits during the Pandemic." *CNN*. May 28, 2020. https://www.cnn.com/2020/05/28/economy/unemployment-benefits-coronavirus/index.html.

Made in the USA
Columbia, SC
10 August 2020

15033525R00109